HIDDEN HISTORY *of* STURGEON BAY

Heidi Hodges and Kathy Steebs

Published by The History Press
Charleston, SC
www.historypress.net

First published 2018

Manufactured in the United States

ISBN 9781467119702

Library of Congress Control Number: 2018936075

Notice: The information in this book is true and complete to the best of our knowledge. It is offered without guarantee on the part of the authors or The History Press. The authors and The History Press disclaim all liability in connection with the use of this book.

This book is dedicated to

Miss Miller and Chan Harris
Fred and Gordon Hodges
Scott and Wil Steebs

and

Keta Steebs
a friend and mentor to both of us, but she only trusted one of us with her ice.

Contents

Contents

Preface

We imagine Keta Steebs and Chan Harris would be pleased. Chan Harris was the longtime owner and editor of the *Door County Advocate*. And Keta was a star reporter on staff.

The staff of the paper was tight—like family. When I joined in 1987, the *Advocate* had expanded from the original triumvirate of Chan, Jim Robertson and Doug Larson to a full newsroom, advertising department and production crew. In the 1950s, those three and their support staff led the paper out of some very bleak days following the murder of Chan's parents. Each addition to the staff was warmly welcomed in.

I came on the scene in 1987 as the *Resorter Reporter* photography intern, taking photos for a special summer section aimed at promoting tourist activities around the county. I shot pictures of the festivals and fun activities and wrote a weekly column.

Chan was the editor who hired me for this dream position, but I came to regard him as almost a grandfather—a grandfather who had the uncanny ability to spot, at a glance, every spelling or grammatical error I made.

Brash, funny Keta worked at a desk in the corner, wearing her trademark wig and smoking cigarettes as she typed away at her stories—hard-hitting news pieces that often ruffled feathers. She also churned out feature stories and kindly profiles at a steady rate. She was well known in the county and far beyond.

She quickly recognized my youthful eagerness with my new job and took me under her wing. Chan educated me, Keta supported me and the rest of the staff adopted me. In 1989, I was officially hired as a full-time staffer.

Kathy and I—coauthors of this book you are holding—met at a dinner party Keta held at her home in the late '80s. Kathy was with her future husband, Keta's son Scott. It was a great evening with food and wine and laughter. More party than dinner—it was Keta's style.

Kathy and Scott moved to Milwaukee, where Scott worked as a teacher and Kathy as a technical writer. Our paths occasionally crossed.

In 2000, Scott and Kathy moved back to Door County. As the years progressed, Kathy and I became great friends and enjoyed a number of fun coincidences: we share the same birthday and year. Our sons are the same age. We ended up working together with the *Door County Magazine*—which is under the umbrella of the *Advocate*.

And we are neighbors.

We have both been very keen on learning about and researching local history, so it seemed perfect that we would team up to write this book.

Chan Harris died in 1998 and Keta Steebs in 2013. While we miss them terribly, we feel they would be awfully proud of our efforts with this book. Both Keta and Chan were ardent supporters of Door County and Sturgeon Bay.

There were so many stories to tell, it was hard to pick. Sturgeon Bay provided us a deep well to draw from. Were there more on our list? Oh, yes, but these were the ones that called to us, the ones that felt more *hidden* in our history.

We have a lot of folks we want to thank for their help in researching the stories and their contributions to the illustrations: Dr. Victoria Tashjian, Tamara Thomsen, Nyla Small, Susie Woldt, Tom and Kathy Anschutz, June Larson, Nancy Aten, Scott Steebs and Wil Steebs. We are indebted to the Door County Maritime Museum, the National Archives in Chicago and the Door County Historical Museum.

We want to thank the *Door County Magazine* and Gannett for allowing us to repurpose several stories that originally ran in different issues of the magazine.

And we want to thank our family and friends, who have let us put in the hours needed to complete this work. These stories need to be told and remembered, to keep our little city's history alive.

And, of course, we want to thank Chan and Keta.

Because without them, our paths would have been quite different.

PART I

PEOPLE

The Character of Sturgeon Bay

Bertha Falk

Widowed Immigrant Finds a New Life

Bertha Helena Falk was out of options.

It was the mid-1800s, and her homeland of Norway could no longer produce enough food to feed its growing population. Her husband, Jorgen, a fisherman, had been lost at sea. With four children under the age of ten to feed and few opportunities for employment, Bertha made a drastic decision.

Joining the ranks of approximately one-third of her fellow Norwegians who left their homeland in search of a better life, Bertha and her children fled. They boarded the schooner *Ebenezer* and set sail for America.

The *Ebenezer* was one of Norway's smallest emigrant sailing vessels—capable of carrying only seventy-five passengers. Steerage accommodations meant Bertha had to bring her own food and cooking utensils and stand in line at the galley every day, waiting for her turn to cook.

Accommodations were tight; she and her children shared sleeping quarters with all but three passengers. (Only one family aboard the *Ebenezer* could afford a cabin.) The Falks likely shared a family bunk, built of rough boards, outfitted with straw bedding and located between the upper deck and the cargo hold. Considering the accommodations, it was likely a rolling cesspool of seasickness, frustration and fear.

But what was ahead would hopefully be better than what was left behind.

Settling a New Community

Despite her compelling story, Bertha is not a well-known Door County settler. There are no parks or roads named for her. No surviving letters or diaries exist detailing her life. Even though she was one of the first white female settlers, early Door County historians Charles I. Martin and Hjalmar R. Holand barely mention her.

Perhaps this is because men were the stars of most each and every story. Women were incidental. Early Door County newspapers kept to this standard as well—with women featured only in marriage announcements, obituaries, church picnic recaps and stories about socializing with relatives. Had it not been for a 1928 *Green Bay Gazette* article written about her son John, Bertha's story would have died with her.

According to the article, Bertha's young family was traveling to the new country as part of a larger group that included nine others who also made the arduous journey from Stavanger, Norway, to Green Bay.

A passenger list for the schooner *Ebenezer* reveals this voyage also included Door County settlers Salvi and Marthe Salvison—later anglicized to Solway—and the Wathne family (Zacharias, Gabriel and Malene), who, according to Holand's *History of Door County, Wisconsin*, then traveled from Green Bay to Door County with the Reverend A.M. Iverson, founder of the Moravian congregation in Ephraim. It is likely that Bertha and her family were part of this group of pioneer Norwegian Moravians.

The Moravians originally planned to settle in the Green Bay area, but in 1852, they decided to search for land on the Door Peninsula instead. Four members of their group, including Salvi Solway and Louis Klinkenberg, chose to settle in the vicinity of Sturgeon Bay rather than follow the rest of the congregation to Ephraim.

At that time, according to the article, Bertha's eight-year-old son, John, accompanied Louis Klinkenberg to the site of what is now Sturgeon Bay, where they found "nobody but Indians."

Hardship quickly found the group of settlers. Even though the early historical writings do not usually mention wives and children by name, we know from Charles Martin's *The History of Door County*, that Salvi Solway's wife, Marthe, died soon after arriving in Door County and was the first white woman buried in Sturgeon Bay.

STARTING OVER AGAIN

In the 1850s, homesteading in Door County meant clearing the land of timber and building log cabins with materials at hand. Everyday supplies could only be purchased in the more settled area of Green Bay, and the only way to travel there was via boat or on foot. Roughing it was a part of everyday life.

The Preemption Act of 1841 allowed pioneer squatters to purchase public lands from the U.S. government before it was offered for public sale. To qualify, the squatter had to be the head of household—a man over the age of twenty-one or a widow—a citizen of the United States or intending to become naturalized. Hopefuls also had to reside on the property for at least fourteen months, continually making improvements.

Yet almost as soon as the widowed Bertha settled on her new homestead, she lost it to a Mr. Crandall.

Illustration of Bertha Falk dismantling her cabin after her land was preempted. *Illustration by Susie Woldt. Courtesy of* Door County Magazine.

Left: Bertha's second husband, Salvi (Solway) Salvison's headstone at Bayside Cemetery in Sturgeon Bay. *Courtesy of Heidi Hodges.*

Below: Bertha Falk Solway's headstone at Bayside Cemetery in Sturgeon Bay. *Courtesy of Heidi Hodges.*

Evidently, this Crandall was able to jump her claim before Bertha could prove she met all of the preemption qualifications. It is easy to imagine this single, immigrant mother at the end of her rope. Perhaps angry and unwilling to concede any more, the plucky matriarch tore down her cabin and sailed it up the bay to another piece of land in what is now Sevastopol.

But that isn't the end of Bertha's story.

Both Holand and Martin record that the newly widowed Salvi Solway and Bertha Falk were married around the time she resettled. In fact, they were the first couple married in Sturgeon Bay. (The officiant was Robert Graham.) In addition to their combined eight children, Bertha and Salvi had at least three more children together.

Salvi's obituary in the 1886 *Door County Advocate* mentions the preemption and loss of land. Although there is no mention of Bertha taking her cabin apart piece by piece and rafting it to a new location, it does mention the move to Sevastopol township. Whether it was Bertha alone who preempted the land as a widow or she did it together with second husband Salvi, it is clear that the land to which they eventually moved in Sevastopol played an important role in their lives and the lives of their descendants—who still own it today.

In the early 1900s, the Solway descendants built a new house and dining hall on the property and began operating Sunnyside Resort, which became a favorite spot of tourists from St. Louis who returned every summer for years.

Bertha Helena Falk Solway died on December, 26, 1903, at eighty-six years old. According her obituary, Bertha "made many friends, by whom she will be greatly missed, as she was a favorite with all."

What the obituary doesn't say is that despite losing her first husband, making a transatlantic journey on a cramped boat with four young kids in tow and losing her land in her new country, she held on. She held on to her cabin, her hopes for a better life and her courageous spirit.

And despite hardship difficult to imagine today, she did what she set out to do.

She survived.

Lum Sam Leaves an Impression on Sturgeon Bay

He wasn't the first. And he wouldn't be the last. But Lum Sam held the distinction of operating Sturgeon Bay's Chinese laundry longer than any of his fellow laundrymen, from 1906 until 1917—according to the *Door County Democrat.*

Hoo Ching opened Sturgeon Bay's first Chinese laundry after Wah Kee, a fellow laundryman from Escanaba, appealed to Sturgeon Bay mayor E.S. Minor regarding the viability of such a business in the city. In a letter dated October 19, 1894, Mayor Minor reported that he felt that it was a worthwhile venture, since most laundry work was sent out to Green Bay and that "a great number of people" visited Sturgeon Bay during the summer season and would "furnish much work."

So began a long venture in Sturgeon Bay, with laundrymen of Chinese descent coming and going on a fairly regular basis. Following Hoo Ching were Ching Chang, George Yung, Ching Chow, Charley Bong and Sam Wing—just to name a few—but Lum Sam outlasted them all.

During a time when prejudice against Chinese immigrants was high—the Chinese Exclusion Act, which prohibited any new immigration of Chinese workers, was signed into law by President Chester A. Arthur in 1882—Sturgeon Bay was not immune to this prejudice. Although the *Door County Democrat* cast a more favorable light on the potential opening of the Chinese laundry than did other local newspapers, it still made some missteps. Their headline detailing the piece about the mayor's invitation read, "The Chinee Are Coming," and the same issue included an article titled "The Heathen Chinee," discussing the mysteries of Chinese characters on laundry tickets.

Despite this anti-Chinese sentiment, Lum Sam seemed to thrive during his time in Sturgeon Bay—he was often mentioned in the local newspapers with comments not only related to his business but to his personal merit as well. In November 1916, the *Door County News* published the sad news that one of Lum Sam's sons had died over the summer.

Lum Sam was also a loyal employer. When one of his employees, Mary Schmidtke, was arrested on suspicion of adultery, he posted $500 for her bail—with the understanding that she would gratefully continue to work for him. Unfortunately, Schmidtke immediately skipped town with her lover. Lum Sam was out the money—that is, until six months later, when authorities in another Wisconsin town responded to a call of domestic abuse and discovered the lovers. Schmidtke was returned to the Sturgeon Bay jail, and Lum Sam's $500 bail money was returned. The *Sturgeon Bay Advocate* reported that Lum Sam "felt great joy" that Schmidtke was apprehended, as he had "lost faith in the feminine sex entirely" after she jumped bail and skipped out on her job at the laundry.

But perhaps the most interesting story published in local newspapers about Lum Sam was an account of him standing up for himself against an injustice and winning a lawsuit against a local justice of the peace. According to the *Sturgeon Bay Advocate* in April 1915, Lum Sam brought a suit against Henry Reynolds, the local magistrate, claiming that Reynolds had borrowed fifty dollars from Lum Sam and, after repaying only fifteen, tore up the promissory note. Reynolds claimed he had paid the note in full and was within his rights to destroy it. After a change of venue to Justice Simpson's court in the township of Sturgeon Bay (rather than the city, which was under Justice Reynold's jurisdiction) and hearing the arguments on both sides, Justice Simpson ruled in favor of Lum Sam. The *Advocate* further reported that Reynolds "made no fight in Justice court but will appeal to the circuit court." No mention was made of an appeal in subsequent newspapers of that year.

At the end of 1916, Lum Sam decided to return to China. Although Lum Sam was an American citizen, his wife and twelve-year-old son still resided in China. He said it was his intent to return to Sturgeon Bay with both wife and son. Before he left, he asked the *Door County Democrat* to publish the following note: "Good People Sturgeon Bay: Lum Sam gone to China. Lum Sam like Sturgeon Bay. By and by come back. So good bye. See again. —Lum Sam"

LUM SAM GOING TO CHINA

Local Landryman For Eleven Years Leaves Next Week For His Old Home In Hong Kong.

Lum Sam, Sturgeon Bay's laundryman for eleven years, leaves either Monday or Tuesday for his old home in Hong Kong, China, to remain a year or longer. During his absence his cousin, Lam Tun, of Chicago, will run the laundry. Lam Tun was here last week, returning to Chicago Saturday and will be back here Monday. He is 30 years old.

Two years ago Lum Sam's mother died and since then five other members of the family have passed away. Lum Sam's son, Lum Lou, died on August 15. The young Chinaman had been working in a Chinese bank in Quebec, Canada, and returned but a few months before he died.

Lum Sam is going back to China to re-bury his mother. It is the custom of the Chinese to unearth their dead after the body has been buried two years. If flesh still remains on the bones the body is reburied, but if the bones are barren of flesh they are taken from the grave and placed in an urn, which is then taken to some place which is elevated, the Chinese believing that the dead can see.

Lum Sam is a citizen of the United States and has voted here. He was born in San Francisco, his father being employed at the time with a railway company. His father took the family back to China and twelve years ago Lum Sam returned to America, staying in New York a year and then coming to Sturgeon Bay where he has been since. Lum Sam, who is 48 years old, has married twice. His first wife died but his second wife is living in Hong Kong and they have a son twelve years old. He expects to bring them back here when he returns.

Lum Sam said he "no like to go to China," and "me like it here fine"—"summer time lots or fun—go baseball boys to Oconto and all over"—"Just like home here and me come back."

Lum Sam's Farewell.

Lum Sam, local laundryman for twelve years, left Monday for his old home in China. He had been at Oconto the week previous on a business trip where he had also been interested with a relative in a laundry and had closed up his affairs there. He has turned over his business here to Lam Pong, a cousin from Chicago.

Lum Sam requested The Democrat to publish the following card:

Good People Sturgeon Bay:

Lum Sam gone to China. Lum Sam like Sturgeon Bay. By and by come back. So good bye. See again. LUM SAM.

LUM SAM REACHES CHINA SAFELY

Letter Says He Is Now Busy With the Domestic Affairs.

Lum Sam, local laundryman, finally arrived at his old home in China. His letter telling of his safe arrival is dated March 27 and reached Sturgeon Bay on April 24. His letter follows:

80 Des Voeux Road W. (1st pr.)
Hongkong, China,
27 March, 1917.

Dear sir:

Six weeks have passed since I departed from you on the 12th of Feb., and on the 20th of March I reached Hongkong safely.

Now I am busy for the domestic affairs. But after an interval I shall go there and hope to see you again.

Hoping to hear from you soon,
Your friend,
LUM SAM.

Domestic affairs Sam refers to evidently are concerned with the reburial of his mother according to Chinese custom. When Sam returns to Sturgeon Bay his wife will probably accompany him. She formerly lived in California with Sam but when he came to Wisconsin she went back to China.

Newspaper clippings from the *Door County Democrat* regarding Lum Sam's trip back to China. *Above*: November 1916; *Right, top*: December 1916; *Right, bottom*: April 1917. *Courtesy of Door County Library Newspaper Archives.*

Unfortunately, Lum Sam would never see Sturgeon Bay again. After safely reaching Hong Kong in March 1917, Lum Sam fell ill and died within forty-eight hours of his arrival—before he was able to reunite with his wife and child.

Although his cousin Lum Tun and others made attempts to run the Chinese laundry during the next few years, none was as successful as Lum Sam. In 1920, the *Door County Advocate* reported that the Chinese laundry, "one of Sturgeon Bay's oldest businesses," was closing its doors and that from now on a "soiled collar will probably be the usual thing."

And so ended the era of Chinese laundry in Sturgeon Bay.

The Pioneering Spirit of the Graham Family

In 1854, Sturgeon Bay was still in its infancy—in fact, it hadn't yet acquired an official name. The new community counted among its residents Native Americans, early business opportunists and rough characters from various parts of the world hoping to eke out an existence on its unspoiled land. Wild, old-growth forests populated much of its shoreline, which attracted early entrepreneurs of the lumber industry, such as Robert Graham, who helped shape Sturgeon Bay's early history.

Robert's older brother Oliver Perry Graham, who staked the first official claim in Sturgeon Bay in 1849, settled in with his family when there were just a handful of other residents—mostly bachelors—in the area. By the time his brother Robert and Robert's wife, Josephine, arrived in Sturgeon Bay in 1854, there were a few more families, but the majority of the community's two hundred residents were single men working in the community's two lumber mills.

While Oliver Perry and his family eventually moved farther north to Egg Harbor, Robert and Josephine and their eight children sunk down deep roots in Sturgeon Bay and forever became part of the fabric of the community.

Josephine Graham, née Mouton, was born in Cuba in 1828 to parents who were originally from South Carolina. By the 1840s, Josephine's family had returned to the United States, and she eventually settled on Rock Island, Door County's northernmost island. At that time, Rock Island was a thriving community, teeming with fishermen, including the Graham brothers, who were Ohio natives of Scottish descent.

While it is not clear what brought Josephine to this remote island in Lake Michigan, we do know that Josephine and Robert were married there in 1846 and started a family soon after. By the time they moved to the peninsula almost a decade later, Josephine had already given birth to the first five of their eight children: Hugh, Eli, William, Robert and Josephine.

Shortly after relocating his family to the shores of what is now Sturgeon Bay, Robert established himself as one of the leaders of the community. In 1855, he recorded the first plat of Sturgeon Bay—which was briefly called the village of Graham in his honor—and joined the burgeoning timber industry by building his own lumber mill on the shore front, located just north of present day Graham Park.

Unfortunately, the lumber industry was hit hard by the financial Panic of 1857, and all the lumber mills—including the Graham mill—went out of business around that time. Unlike many others associated with the mills, the Grahams did not pick up and leave when the lumbering business failed. Instead, Robert focused on his other endeavors as storekeeper, postmaster and fisherman. During the ensuing years, he wore a variety of hats within the community: justice of the peace, town clerk, school district clerk, real estate agent, shipbuilder and captain of his family's fishing and shipping business.

While living in Sturgeon Bay, Robert and Josephine added three more children to their brood: Joseph, Lucy and Charles. By all accounts, the family was close and worked many of the businesses together. Sons Robert and Eli were early mail carriers when they were as young as eleven and twelve years old, riding mules fifty miles through the woods to pick up and deliver the mail to Green Bay. Hugh, Eli and Joseph all worked in the family fishing business.

Like many pioneers, the family was not untouched by tragedy. By the time of Josephine's death from tuberculosis in 1883 at the age of fifty-five, she had already outlived four of her eight children. In 1870, nine-year-old Charlie, the youngest, drowned in the bay as the result of a boating accident, and Hugh, the eldest, died in 1878 at age thirty from complications following surgery. Two of Josephine's children succumbed to the same disease as she did: son Joseph died in 1880 at the age of twenty-two and daughter Lucy in 1883 (just a month before her mother) at the age of twenty-four.

In 1889, another daughter, Josephine, died from tuberculosis at the age of thirty-six, just seven months after giving birth to her third child. Both daughters, Lucy and Josephine, had taken turns nursing their sick mother, so they likely contracted the disease from her.

Most likely it was Robert himself who unwittingly brought home the illness that would eventually take such a heavy toll on his family. When he died in 1873 at the age of forty-nine, his obituary in the *Door County Advocate* described how Robert contracted the disease in 1860 when the lure of Pike's Peak gold rush drew him to Colorado, where "he was attacked with a fever, from the effects of which he never fully recovered, which undoubtedly hastened his death."

There is little doubt that Robert and Josephine left their mark on the community that they helped create. Although Josephine's obituary is sparse—typical for women during this era—Robert's is full of detail, describing him as "an energetic business man—never idle; of good business habits, strict integrity" and "universally respected by his friends and neighbors." Robert Graham's strong pioneer spirit, many business endeavors and community leadership helped found the city of Sturgeon Bay.

And his wife, Josephine—equally strong in pioneer spirit—was beside him every step of the way.

Founding Father Joseph Harris

The building of this canal, with break wall, would not only open Sturgeon Bay as a harbor of refuge, it would save them [vessels] *a distance of 200 miles each voyage of dangerous navigation and through the "Door" where many noble and valuable vessels and their cargoes are annually lost.*
—Door County Advocate, *January 30, 1864*

While the Civil War raged in the South, Sturgeon Bay had taken up a cause of its own: the building of a ship canal bisecting the peninsula east to west in the burgeoning city of Sturgeon Bay. On a map, it's easy to see the advantage of a canal. The Door Peninsula stretches up into Lake Michigan, separating Green Bay from the main body of Lake Michigan—setting a barrier between developing regions of commerce during a time when shipping was king.

The peninsula, a seventy-mile-long spit of land, was like a wall between the mainland of Wisconsin and the open waters of Lake Michigan, the route to harbors in Milwaukee, Chicago and beyond. Mariners sailing from Green Bay to ports on Lake Michigan had to navigate a stretch of water at the tip of the peninsula dubbed "Death's Door" because of its treacherous currents, powerful winds and obstructing islands.

Even if everything went well with the voyage, the trip around the peninsula added a couple hundred extra miles and a couple extra days of time.

But there was a solution—albeit, a difficult one.

A young Joseph Harris Sr. *Courtesy of the* Door County Advocate.

The building of a shipping canal, bisecting the middle of the peninsula in Sturgeon Bay, would allow ships to avoid the time-consuming and perilous trip around the peninsula and through the Death's Door passage.

As for Sturgeon Bay, a canal would give the city a leg up in this developing area of Wisconsin. With ships passing by—and occasionally lingering in the safe harbor of refuge—the infant city would have the potential to grow into a boom town.

Such was the dream of Joseph Harris Sr.

Harris, an early immigrant to Sturgeon Bay, is widely considered an important founding father for the city, although he had his detractors. Nevertheless, his efforts in the mid-1800s laid the foundation for the city's future.

Born in England in 1813, Harris immigrated to the United States at the age of thirty-six with his wife, Charlotte Singleton. In New York, where he first settled, he worked for the *Evening Register* newspaper and in the real estate business for six years. The couple had five children—Charlotte, Joseph Jr., Elizabeth, Henry and Edith—before his wife, Charlotte, died in 1855.

Joseph Harris soon left New York, journeying to Wisconsin, where he settled in Sturgeon Bay. He called for his children to join him soon after.

Harris made his presence known shortly after he arrived in the small settlement, not yet named Sturgeon Bay. (The larger township was already known as Sturgeon Bay, but the city itself was then known as Otumba.)

Immediately, he became involved. According to Hjalmar Holand's *History of Door County, Wisconsin*, Harris traveled twenty-three miles by foot to Fish Creek to participate in the first meeting of the newly formed Door County Board of Supervisors and was soon elected the county board's first secretary. The town of Sturgeon Bay was the second recognized township after Washington—the island at the northern tip of the peninsula.

In 1859, he married his second wife, Susan Perkins, who hailed from the Wisconsin town of Pensaukee. The two would eventually go on to have five more children, although only two survived, Grace and Arthur Harris.

Joseph Harris held other positions with the county, and in 1864, during the height of the Civil War, he was elected to the state senate. He might have become a footnote in local history if not for two major accomplishments: He founded the *Door County Advocate*, the county's first newspaper (which, in name, survives to this day) and was the impetus behind the eventually successful shipping canal project.

Through his efforts, the two were closely linked together. In the fall of 1861 he and a somewhat reluctant business partner, Myron McCord, founded the *Door County Advocate*. Years later, McCord, remembering the venture, wrote he was less than enthusiastic about the business idea. But Harris's ambition and excitement for the newspaper project was so great that he signed on, albeit temporarily.

In 1902, an *Advocate* article referenced a letter written by McCord, describing those early days of the *Advocate*'s founding:

> *The writer* [Myron McCord] *met Joseph Harris, Sr. by appointment for the purpose of talking over the advisability of establishing a newspaper at Sturgeon Bay. Mr. Harris was very enthusiastic over the project and did not appear to think there was any question of a financial character about the matter. He was completely wrapped up in the idea of setting up Door County and thought a newspaper the one thing needful to accomplish that result.*
>
> *When it was suggested that a newspaper could not be published without quite an outlay of money and that the population of the county was small;*

that the actual outlay for help and blank paper, rent and fuel could not be figured at less than $1000 a year, he was completely perplexed and did not know what to say. He was at that time serving the people in the capacity of county treasurer, receiving, I believe, a salary of $400 a year, and this he required for his own living, and as a matter of course, was compelled to live in a very frugal manner to make both ends meet.

The article goes on to describe how McCord eventually agreed to join the business. He located printing equipment for sale in Shawano, on the other side of Green Bay, and brought it back to Sturgeon Bay via a two-horse sleigh. "I don't think I should have consented to undertake the venture had it not been for the earnestness with which Mr. Harris pleaded," wrote McCord.

While he initially signed on, it wasn't long before McCord decided the newspaper business wasn't in his best interest, so he sold his interest in the venture, while Harris continued as publisher and editor. McCord did note that Harris paid off the debt to him on time and in full.

Harris, apparently, kept good company. McCord went on to serve in Congress and, according to the March 22, 1902 *Advocate*, eventually became governor of the Arizona Territory.

In the early days, the newly founded *Door County Advocate* was a means of delivering war news, international news, advertisements and occasional local tidbits—although surprisingly few local stories. There were letters from local soldiers serving in the war, including Harris's own sons Joseph Jr. and Henry (nicknamed Harry).

Although the first issue of the *Advocate* proclaimed the new paper would be independent in politics and free of personal vendettas, Harris was strongly aligned with the Republican Party of the day. The paper supported President Lincoln and the war effort in patriotic tone. Indeed, after Harris's death in 1889, *Advocate* editor Frank Long wrote in the obituary that Harris was

ardently devoted to the Union cause and did everything in his power to assist the Lincoln administration in suppressing the great insurrection….

He was not satisfied with this manifestation of loyalty, however, but early realized the fact that he must have a newspaper through whose columns he could expound the true gospel of duty and patriotism.

All during the war, Harris and the newspaper advocated for eligible men to sign up and avoid a possible draft. Practically every issue included admonitions for local men to serve their country; stories extolled the "glorious deaths" of union soldiers and the virtues of volunteering for service.

The newspaper may have played a role in Door County's higher-than-average recruitment rates; of the 3,000 residents of the county at the time, 167 joined the Union army. Of that number, 17 died, 17 were wounded and at least 6 were taken prisoner, according to the centennial edition of the *Door County Advocate*, published in 1962.

By September 1864, a draft was in place for the Union, and the paper urged calm acceptance:

> *The Draft is not a very pleasant thing per se. But there is no use in making one's self a fool about it.... The Draft is a necessity of the war. It comes because the war wants soldiers and must have them, or stop. Lincoln didn't get up the war, if some Copperhead did say so. The rebels, with Jeff. Davis at their head, got up the war and Lincoln is trying to put them down and restore the nation; and he is slowly doing it. And he is slowly doing it because it is so large and determined and diabolical. Now, do you want the war to stop by giving up to the rebels and dividing the nation? Go in with the Copperheads and cry peace, while peace means "Confederate Independence" with "original boundaries." War means fighting; and in fighting, somebody has it to do. Will you defend your country or let it go?... Keep cool then; and when the Draft comes, act the philosopher and the man of sense.*

In fact, the newspaper supported Lincoln so strongly that in September 1864, it announced it would stop printing more "trivial" local stories—as few as they had been—in order to offer more space for election information and Lincoln support: "Have patience! After Mr. Lincoln is reelected President (which will be on the 8th day of November next) we will gratify your tastes in the matter. For the present, we have other duties to perform than to write, print or read stories."

While Harris was on the homefront, supporting Lincoln and the war and urging readers to do their duty, two of his sons were fully involved as soldiers. Harris printed occasional letters from his son Harry:

> *A letter from our boy Harry in this week's paper, gives a brief account of the expedition under Col. Bryant. It is the most interesting, as being the first time the boys have had the chance of a tussle with the rebels, and from all we can hear from other sources, it is gratifying to know, that with very*

few casualties on our side, the loss to the rebels was heavy, in killed and wounded, a large number being made to bite the dust.

—Door County Advocate, *May 1864*

Both sons ultimately survived and returned from the war, although Joseph Jr. was wounded in action.

Harris also called for abolition. In many *Advocate* issues, Harris made strong arguments and refuted claims that freed slaves would be unproductive and unmanageable by quoting statistics and studies that supported his antislavery views.

In April 1865, immediately after Lincoln was assassinated, the paper ran an issue with columns separated by thick, black lines as a show of mourning.

Probably one of the most gripping stories in the issues that followed was the blow-by-blow account of the capture and death of accused Lincoln assassin John Wilkes Booth. In breathtaking narrative, derived from other sources and assembled into a story and retold in the *Advocate*, the paper describes the minute details of Booth's last moments, as federal forces surrounded the barn in which he was hiding:

Booth: "I will never surrender. I will never be taken alive."
Lieutenant Baker: "If you don't do so immediately, we will set fire to the barn."
Booth: "Well, my brave boys, prepare a stretcher for me."

The paper goes on to describe the final moments of Booth's life:

Lieutenant Baker pulled out a wisp of hay and lighted it. Within a few minutes the blazing hay lighted up the inside of the barn. Booth was discovered leaning on a crutch, which he threw aside, and with a carbine in his hands, came toward the side where the fire had been kindled, paused, looked at the fire a moment and started toward the door. When in about the middle of the barn, he was shot.

There was a first-person account from Booth's shooter:

I aimed at his body. I did not want to kill him. I took deliberate aim at his shoulder, but my aim was too high. The ball struck him in the head, just below the right ear, and passing through came out about an inch above the left ear. I think he stopped to pick up something just as I fired. That may probably account for his receiving the ball in the head.... I was afraid that if I did not wound him, he would kill some of our men.

After he was wounded, I went into the barn. Booth was lying in a reclining position on the floor I asked him, "Where are you wounded?" He replied, in a feeble voice, his eyeballs glaring with a peculiar brilliancy, "In the head. You have finished me." He was then carried out of the burning building into the open air, where he died about two hours and a-half afterwards. About an hour before he breathed his last, he prayed for us to shoot him through the heart, and thus end his misery. His sufferings seemed to be intense.

Booth, although he could have killed several of our party, seemed to be afraid of fire.... We gave him brandy, and four men went in search of a doctor, whom we found in about four miles from the scene of occurrence. But when the doctor arrived, Booth was dying. He did not talk much after receiving his wound. When asked if he had anything to say, he replied: "I die for my country," and asked those standing by to tell his mother so. He did not deny his crime.

This gripping prose went on for an entire page of a four-page issue that also included news of newly sworn in president Andrew Johnson and national matters pertaining to the assassination. There were also small, biting editorial bits pointing out the irony of Booth being shot in the same bodily location as Lincoln and remarks about Booth's cowardice.

Considering the space devoted to the narrative, it was likely the most important news the paper had printed to that point. And the *Advocate* was likely the only source for county residents to get that news.

Still, local news—even war-related—was treated as an afterthought. Interestingly, in the issue previous to the one describing Booth's capture, there was a one-sentence report, buried in a column of other mundane news, about the death of a nineteen-year-old Door County lad who had died as the result of his war wounds.

After the war, however, the paper began a move toward more day-to-day happenings locally, statewide and nationally—both big news and smaller tidbits. And as Joseph Sr. became more active in politics, Joseph Jr. and Harry took over running the paper.

At that point, Harris turned his attention to the shipping canal in earnest. During the early days of the *Advocate*, in addition to war news, the paper served as a sounding board for Harris's pet project, the Sturgeon Bay shipping canal. Once the war was over, the shipping canal took over as top story. It wasn't a new story, though. The canal was first proposed in 1835 during a federal land survey of Door County.

According to a letter published in the *Advocate* in 1878, a company was formed to establish a canal as early as 1830, but a "financial crash of that year put an end to the project, the land was sold for taxes and the company disbanded." The idea sat idle until 1856, when the state legislature granted a charter for the construction of a canal, but a recession halted plans and the charter allowed to expire. As noted in an 1879 *Advocate* report, Harris said that he himself took up the "old abandoned project for cutting a ship canal through from the head of Sturgeon Bay into Lake Michigan."

Harris picked up the baton and began his campaign for the canal in 1860, although there was little support for the idea at first. But, from Little Sturgeon, a burgeoning community just south of Sturgeon Bay, the influential F.B. Gardner joined forces with Harris, and the two worked together to garner attention and support for the project. (A township in southern Door County was later named for Gardner.) Harris also secured support from other state and national politicians.

Even during the war, Harris had been working to keep the canal project in the forefront. Eventually, the canal took up a prominent position in the paper—almost every issue featured a bit of news or an editorial-style encouragement of the proposed project.

Harris's arguments for the canal met with ridicule and skepticism. According to Holand's *History of Door County*, Harris was surrounded by "men of small means and little insight and…laughed at as a dreamer." None of this deterred him.

After four years of Harris's work to gain support, a new charter was issued to the Sturgeon Bay and Lake Michigan Ship Canal and Harbor Company to construct the canal. But that was just the first step. That same year, 1864, Harris was elected to the Wisconsin legislature, representing Door, Oconto, Outagamie and Shawano Counties. As reported in the 1864 *Advocate*, "With our senator, there is no such word as fail, if perseverance and indomitable energy will do it, it will be done and there can be no doubt of his success."

In his new position of influence, Harris doubled down on his efforts, including traveling to Washington to obtain a 200,000-acre federal land grant—land located in other areas to provide material and capital to keep the canal project afloat. But it was an uphill battle. Harris didn't exactly get a warm reception at the House of Representatives in 1865; he was told by Representative Walter McIndoe that 200,000 acres of Wisconsin timber was "worth more than a million dollars." Harris was warned not to ask for more than 50,000 acres.

But he pressed on. The requested 200,000 acres passed the Senate but lost in the House by two votes.

Harris was undaunted. In 1866, he petitioned Congress yet again, and this time, the measure passed. President Andrew Johnson approved the bill on April 10, 1866. Harris lost reelection to the Wisconsin State Senate in 1866, so he returned to his supporters to form the canal company and begin work. At this point, Harris was confident that "the hardest part of my labors were over" and that work would promptly begin on the canal.

But his confidence didn't last long. During a trip to New York in 1868 to meet with the president and vice president of the company, William B. Ogden and Alexander Mitchell, respectively, Harris was told that a mere 200,000-acre land grand wasn't enough to induce investors to join the canal company, and furthermore, the land Congress had already granted was "worthless."

They urged Harris to return to Congress for another 200,000 acres. Harris did, and he worked for several years for the additional acreage. In the meanwhile, the original land grant expired twice, but Harris managed to renew it each time, "after much stress and anxiety." Then, Harris's efforts were dealt a blow: Congress voted to abolish the practice of awarding land grants.

Harris described the situation in Door County's *Expositor Independent* newspaper in 1879:

> *For the first 10 years of my labors, I stood alone, unaided by any of the wealthy corporations who lent me their names to place in the charter of incorporation, but who for want of faith in its ultimate success, would advance no funds to help me carry it along. They gave me plenty of cheering words to go on and get more lands from Congress, but nothing more; and I then realized that if the Canal were ever to be built, there must be but one course for me to pursue; that I must push on and do the best I could for means to carry me along.*

And so he did. It was back to the drawing board for Harris, who, by the early 1870s, was working as secretary for Wisconsin representative Philetus Sawyer in Washington, D.C.

Sawyer, acting chairman of the Committee on River and Harbor Appropriations, was working on a bill to improve Wisconsin's rivers and

Prepping land for the Sturgeon Bay Ship Canal. *Courtesy of Door County Maritime Museum.*

harbors. At Harris's urging, Sawyer included creating a harbor of refuge in Sturgeon Bay and a survey of the proposed canal route.

The harbor of refuge funds would be as valuable as a second land grant, he theorized.

But the project was dealt yet another blow. The original 200,000-acre land grant, for whatever it was worth, was located in Kewaunee, Brown, Oconto and Marinette Counties. Unfortunately, the land lay in the path of the Great Fire of 1871, the same fire that destroyed Chicago and killed over 1,500 people in northern Wisconsin.

The result was a virtual halt in the sale of the canal bonds—money that was essential for the work to begin. Also, lumber thieves had been at work, stripping whatever valuable timber was left. But there was some relief from Congress, in the form of disaster relief money and "trespass funds." The thieves were made to pay $40,000, and Congress approved another $40,000.

By May 1872, the canal company investors finally had the confidence to add $75,000 to the project, and work was ready to commence. Construction finally began in 1872. On July 8 of that year, the first shovelful of dirt was dug, with work continuing for over a decade until the canal was large enough to be operational.

GROWING MISTRUST

But there was a growing sense of mistrust and resentment toward Harris in Sturgeon Bay and the county.

About one quarter of the work had been completed by fall of 1872, when another economic downturn halted progress.

During the next three years, work on the canal came to a virtual standstill. It was during this time that the people of Sturgeon Bay became restless and accused Harris of raising funds for the canal and pocketing the money.

In 1873, a competing newspaper—the first of several in an epic newspaper rivalry—started up. And with every issue of the new *Expositor* came jabs, complaints and editorials about Harris, derisively calling him "The Senior," "Sr." and, on occasion, "the little man in black."

By this time, Harris had sold his interest in the *Advocate* to Frank Long, who had worked as a printer's devil when the paper first published. Long continued in the same political tradition as Harris, and Joseph Jr.'s son Harry continued to work for the newspaper.

Joseph Harris Sr.'s influence in the county and his past connection to the paper were constantly part of the *Expositor*'s story repertoire. Editor George Pinney left no stone unturned:

> *We advise the little man in black not to make a fool of himself by writing in a great passion, even if the provocation is great. He should turn over a "bran new"* [sic] *leaf and take a noble pride in exhibiting the dignified courtesy of a gentleman, as well as the forbearance of a christian. Remember, the more you gloat over the severity of what you have written, the more of an ass you will be for publishing it.*
>
> —Expositor, *November 7, 1873*

And the paper even expounded on typesetting errors in the *Advocate*, often at length (despite having several of its own):

> *Somebody ought to present the editor with a dictionary.*
>
> —Expositor, *November 21, 1873*

And this classic:

> *Complaints about "that sidewalk on Cedar Street" have become chronic with our neighbor the* Advocate. *Do they find the navigation difficult between the saloons?*

In the 1962 centennial edition of the *Advocate*, then-editor Chandler Harris, great-grandson of Joseph Sr., wrote:

> *There was no love lost between Pinney and Harry Harris. Harry wrote of his rival: "...he is such an inveterate liar that when he becomes an inhabitant of the regions below, he will swear he likes it while suffering the torments of the damned."*
>
> *The feud almost cost Pinney his life. When the July 4th, 1878 canal celebration was held, the* Expositor *ridiculed it, probably because Harry's father Joseph had been the chief force behind the canal project. Judge Rufus Wright, emcee at the celebration, took offense at the* Expositor*'s coverage and when a few days later the judge emerged from a saloon and encountered Pinney, he pulled a revolver and took a shot at the local journalist. Fortunately, he missed.*

In 1873, the *Expositor* took Harris to task for his support of a certain political candidate—in favor of another candidate in the same Republican Party. And when Harris's candidate failed, the *Expositor* was merciless:

> *The unscrupulousness of his course has been well known here, and had become unbearable. This year, the people have refused to be longer led by this man, Harris....The people have learned the world moves as usual, even though they have dethroned a dictator.*
>
> *And now Mr. J. Harris Sr., one word more in your ear and we will let you drop from the point of our pen into the oblivion, which, as a politician, you so richly merit.*
>
> *You have the supreme satisfaction of knowing that your overweening ambition has caused you political ruin, and that from this disastrous failure, there is no recovery. Hereafter, the people will not bow to your royal highness nor ask you whom they may elect to represent them in any department of government.*

But, of course, it would not be the last word. The *Expositor* continued to be the voice of opposition against Harris and called into question practically every statement made in the *Advocate* regarding the canal project, of which Harris continued to be the leading supporter.

Slowly but surely, work on the canal started up again and progressed. By the end of the 1873 work season, the "cut" was one-quarter completed.

Construction on the Sturgeon Bay Shipping Canal began on July 8, 1872. *Courtesy of Door County Maritime Museum.*

Work progresses on the Sturgeon Bay Ship Canal. In 1879, the canal was finished enough for the first sailing vessel to travel through. *Courtesy of the Door County Maritime Museum.*

Then, a nationwide depression struck. And work stopped for three years.

As with many large projects, there was controversy. Some questioned the canal's ownership by a private company. The *Expositor* often raised red flags about the company's demands for land in order to complete the work. And it questioned the presumed lack of progress.

> *The* Advocate *says the Canal has been pushed into the bank five hundred feet this season, and at that rate of progress "it will take three years and six months to complete it." Somebody should present that editor with an Arithmetic* [sic]. *There is a mile and a quarter yet to dig, and the* Advocate *says five hundred feet a year will complete it in three years and six months.*
>
> *Will some school boy correct the* Advocate*'s figures?"*

The public responded with frustration and, in some cases, outright anger. But subsequent investigations showed that the canal project's stunted progress was a victim of the depression, and eventually, more of the promised land was turned over to the canal company.

A sailing vessel makes its way through the Sturgeon Bay Ship Canal. *Courtesy of Door County Maritime Museum.*

On June 28, 1878, only two feet of earth separated Sturgeon Bay and Lake Michigan. The project superintendent dug this out with a shovel, and the current widened the cut. Finally, water flowed freely through the canal.

The first ship to go through was a rowboat with project engineer Captain Casgrain at the helm. Six days later, canal workers and the entire city of Sturgeon Bay celebrated the joining together of the waters of Lake Michigan and Green Bay.

There was still more work to do. It wasn't until 1879 that the canal was capable of handling large sailing vessels. The schooner *America* was the first three-masted vessel to be towed through the canal.

A decade later, the yearly number of ships passing through the canal blossomed to nearly four thousand.

There was a toll collected to pass through the canal towed by a tug. Captains figured out a way around the high fees by tying up together and going in as one. Eventually, as tolls increased, ship captains once again began making the voyage around the Death's Door to avoid the canal.

So, the demand for a free canal began to grow.

Ship captains found a method to decrease toll charges by hooking incoming vessels together and coming in under tow as one. When tolls increased, ships began sailing around the peninsula to avoid the canal. In 1893, the canal was sold to the federal government and became free of tolls. *Courtesy of Door County Maritime Museum.*

In the early 1890s, the canal management was investigated for not filing annual operating reports. Charges were filed—and counter-charges. In the end, no evidence of criminal activity was discovered. But it was clear that the time had come for the canal to become a structure free of tolls and private management. In 1893, the federal government purchased the canal for $103,000.

With a U.S. Coast Guard Station at the mouth of the canal, the government set about improving, widening and creating a harbor with a breakwall. After these improvements, newer and larger steamships could use the canal as well.

Today, commercial and recreational ships alike continue to rely on the canal for quick and safe passage between the lake and bay. In early winter, one-thousand-foot freighters thread their way through the narrow passage to Fincantieri Bay Shipbuilding for "winter lay-up" and annual repairs.

Hikers can enjoy the recreational park area created when the canal was built that runs alongside its sandy banks. A region of ecologically and geographically delicate ridges and swales near the mouth of the canal area is also managed by a local land trust conservation.

THE NEWSPAPER FEUDS

As for the newspaper situation, the path to today's *Advocate* was just as complicated as the one leading to the completion of the canal.

The *Advocate* survived during tough times, largely due to its contract with the county to print legal notices. "Legals were the chief source of revenue in those days, and the paper that got them was the paper that survived," wrote Chan Harris in 1962. The *Advocate* had the contracts; the *Expositor* didn't. As such, the *Expositor* closed its doors on February 26, 1886.

Owing to their long-standing feud, the *Advocate* couldn't let the *Expositor*'s death go unremarked upon. It featured a lengthy, legendary obituary for the paper, citing "paralysis of the brain and pocket, weakness of the spinal column, flatulence, swelled head, hard times, universal contempt, mismanagement, stupidity, ignorance, general debility and natural cussedness" as the cause of its death.

Between the time of the *Expositor*'s demise and the late 1920s, another newspaper war in the city emerged as new publications sprang up, editors and owners switched allegiances and names changed. Newspapers merged, and in fact, for a brief time in 1892–93, there were two publications called the *Democrat.*

Each paper and editor had its own projects and political focus—and some papers were created solely to oppose positions held by another paper. For a time, colorful *Advocate* editor D.S. Crandall opposed extending a railroad line into Door County. So, a new newspaper backed by pro-railroad supporters started up, and eventually, it hired Crandall away from the *Advocate.* This was a move beneficial for both parties, as the *Advocate* was beginning to get a reputation as "obstructionist," wrote Chan Harris in 1962.

Oddly enough, in his new position, Crandall immediately changed his tune on the subject of the railroad, and as Chan Harris noted, "Crandall lashed out at the *Advocate* as if he never made a dime there."

At one point in the late 1800s, the *Advocate* began to lose money, and stockholders looked for a new buyer. Joseph Harris Jr. stepped up. He changed the *Advocate*'s name to the the *Republican* and, a year later, sold it to his son, J.E. Harris, who changed the paper's name (and politics) to the *Democrat.* At the same time, George Pinney's son J.J. started *his* own newspaper, also called the *Democrat.* For the time both papers existed, Harris's paper was nicknamed "The Little Democrat."

If you are confused, you aren't alone. Maps and flow charts exist to document the history of Door County's early newspapers. It was also confusing for residents and readers of the day, who were startled by sudden changes in their papers' politics and stances.

In the end, Harris's little *Democrat* went out of business, and Pinney bought the subscription list. The remaining *Democrat* provided "superior coverage of public affairs," Chan Harris wrote in 1962. When J.J. Pinney died in March 1910, the paper's employees purchased the paper and formed the Door County Publishing Company, which went on to purchase what was left of the *Advocate* and publish under the *Door County Advocate* banner.

Today, the *Advocate* remains the county's official paper, with occasional competitors—newspapers, shoppers and other publications—making their mark in the county.

But it all started with Joseph Harris's first newspaper, created to support the Union and his local canal project. With both ultimately successful endeavors, his legacy left a profoundly lasting mark on Sturgeon Bay.

The Long, Hard Journey of Peter Custis

Peter Custis's story starts with slavery. But it ends in Sturgeon Bay, with freedom.

Born in Virginia in 1842 (or maybe 1846—the accounts are in conflict) to Jim and Hannah Custis, Peter Custis's childhood was one of slave labor on the James Custis plantation in Williamsburg. Peter, like his father, was given the plantation owner's last name, as was the custom.

According to a 1928 *Green Bay Press Gazette* story about Peter, plantation owner James Custis "also owned Peter's father and mother and two uncles, and in later years acquired more slaves until the outbreak of the war at which time he had about 200 negroes in his possession."

Young Peter herded cows and hogs until he was strong enough to do heavier work. In his later years, Custis recalled that his treatment was not brutal, but he did say slaves were not allowed to learn to read or write. "Any slave caught disobeying the order was subject to from nine to fifteen lashes with a raw hide whip. Every possible means was used to keep the negroes in an ignorant state," reported the *Press Gazette*.

While Peter was never sold, his mother was placed on auction three times, according to the *Press Gazette*. Local historian Marlene Allen, who gathered recollections and information on Custis, said that at a 1928 program held at the Sturgeon Bay High School, Peter described watching his mother sold, loaded on a wagon and sent to another plantation. It was the last time he ever saw her.

During the same speech, he talked about being a stable boy for Abraham Lincoln, but those claims have been difficult to verify, since it was the only publicly recorded mention.

"The moral conditions among the slaves were much higher than the white people in the South at that time, according to Custis' version," according to the 1928 *Press Gazette*, describing marriage ceremonies the slaves performed, using slave preachers who had secretly learned to read.

Custis had an understandably dim view of the southern whites, indicated by other things he reportedly said. "The negro preachers were and always have been better talkers than their white bretheren," the story quoted Custis as having said.

Prior to the Civil War, Custis recalled that northerners mingled with slaves and told them of the advantages of freedom. "The slaves were fully aware of the approaching calamity, and although their sentiment was with the northern army, they lacked arms and ammunition as well as leadership and were forced to remain and till southern soil," noted the *Press Gazette* story.

When the Civil War broke out, Peter Custis was nearly eighteen years old and was pressed into service.

"He told people here [in Sturgeon Bay] that he worked at three different [Confederate] hospitals," noted Dr. Victoria Tashjian. Tashjian, a professor of history at St. Norbert's College in DePere, Wisconsin, has extensively researched Custis's life.

Custis was in Richmond, Danville and then Petersburg, Virginia, to build breastworks—temporary fortifications. He was at the Battle of Petersburg—a siege that lasted from June 1864 through March 1865—when Custis and about fifty other slaves were captured by Union forces.

"Early in the war, enslaved people [who were captured by the Union] would be turned back over to owners," Tashjian said. But as the war continued, escaped or captured slaves were retained and called contraband of war. Some became soldiers in the Union army, while others filled servile positions. That is what happened to Custis, Tashjian explained.

"Each officer in the Union army had the privilege of taking a negro slave as a valet," the *Press Gazette* story reported. Custis served Colonel Clement E. Warner of Madison, Wisconsin, in the Thirty-Sixth Wisconsin regiment. He remained with Colonel Warner throughout the remainder of the war, caring for horses and serving the colonel.

At one point, according to the *Press Gazette*, Custis reportedly saved a Union soldier's life by securing aid for the wounded man. The man, it turned out, was from nearby Manitowoc, Wisconsin.

According to the recollections collected by Marlene Allen, Peter Custis claimed to have worked in Abraham Lincoln's stables for a time, but there is no official record of that service. Tashjian explained that the timeline of his service allowed little time for it, except while his Union officer, Colonel Warner, was suffering in a hospital with a severe wound. So, although there is no record of Custis's service under Lincoln, it is possible he did help in the stables for a short time.

Records show Custis returned to Dane County, Wisconsin, with Colonel Warner, who was severely wounded in the war and had his left arm amputated. For several years, Custis worked on central Wisconsin farms. For one year, he lived in Sun Prairie with Dr. Elizah Woodward, who had been a surgeon with the army during the Civil War. While with Woodward, Custis attended school for a year and learned to read and write.

Then, around 1868, he set out for Green Bay.

History often shows the *who* and *when* of events that happened but less often the *why*. Why Custis left Dane County is subject to speculation, but census records show he lived with an African American family, the Smiths, in Preble, Wisconsin, in 1870. Later census records show he continued to live in the Green Bay area, but on his own.

More dates and places come in fast succession in census and other formal records: in 1884, he married Leonia Bell. In 1885, he was still in Green Bay and probably welcomed his first son. (Census records indicate two males and one female in the household.)

At some point—possibly in 1885 or thereabouts—Custis and his family moved to Sturgeon Bay.

In 1889, the first of many tragedies struck the Custis household. Leonia gave birth to a stillborn son after a breech delivery. A week later, Leonia died, perhaps a result from the difficult birth.

By that time, however, they had two sons, George and Louis, who were two and four years old at the time of their mother's death. Despite Custis's presence, it was unclear with whom the children would live after the tragic loss of their mother, according to Tashjian.

Custis was involved with the local Quakers, who had set up a church on the West Side of Sturgeon Bay. The church indicated it intended to help him with his children.

A May 1890 issue of the *Door County Advocate* made a small mention that Custis spent the previous winter in Milwaukee. Again, the *why* of history was left blank, with speculation he may have left to escape the grief of losing his wife, said Tashjian.

Peter Custis at the Hagen and English Stone Quarry at the mouth of Sturgeon Bay. *Courtesy of Door County Historical Museum.*

But he returned to Sturgeon Bay. In an 1895 census, Custis was listed in a household by himself in the area. At some point, his children were reunited with him; by 1900, the census records that George, then thirteen, and Louis, fifteen, were living with him once again in Sturgeon Bay. By then, Louis was working at the Hagen and English stone quarry in town, and George was attending school. Though racism was prevalent in the state, "Wisconsin did allow African Americans to attend public school," Tashjian explained.

Another interesting fact recorded in the 1900 census, which was compiled in June of that year, is mention of a fourth member of the Custis household—twenty-four-year-old Julia VanDoozer, a white woman from Algoma.

VanDoozer, the daughter of an area fire or police chief, married Custis on October 11, 1900.

In short order, their family began to grow, with five more children. But, as Tashjian discovered, the family had a particularly hard time.

In 1901, their daughter Hannah was born, followed in January 1902 by another daughter, Melissa Irene. In 1903, their son Arthur was born. But tragedy struck in May of that year when Arthur succumbed to what was declared bronchitis. On July 4, 1903, young Melissa Irene also died of bronchitis. And then, in August of that year, George, Custis's son from his first wife, died.

"The death certificate listed the cause as chronic nephritis, inflammation of the kidneys, that may have been aggravated by alcohol consumption," said Tashjian. In July 1905, Julia gave birth to another daughter, Mellassa Luella.

But in the 1905 census, Peter and Julia appear separately, with each declared the head of their own household. Interestingly, Louis—Peter's surviving son from his first marriage—was listed as living with Julia.

Despite the living arrangements, Julia and Peter remained married.

In February 1906, the seven-month-old Mellassa died of what was reported as enteritis, inflammation of the intestines. It's apparent that Peter and Julia continued their relationship, because on October 28, 1906, Julia gave birth to their fifth child. But the delivery was premature, and the unnamed child died only two hours later.

Then, only four days after the death of her fifth child, Julia died. Her cause of death was listed as "acute pulmonary tuberculosis, asthma and exhaustion after being ill for seven weeks," per Tashjian.

There was more tragedy in store for Peter when, in 1921, his son Louis "was taken to an asylum and said to have been sick due to drinking moonshine," said Tashjian.

Only his daughter Hannah survived and thrived, with perhaps one major misstep along the way. "The White Way Circus—a traveling Chautauqua—came to Sturgeon Bay. Rumor had it that she fell in love with someone in the circus and took off," said Tashjian.

At the time, the *Advocate* wrote of the scandal: Hannah "made a bad choice and will be back," it reported. Indeed, she did return, when her father, Peter, fell ill. Peter Custis ultimately recovered, and Hannah married a man from New York.

By the mid-1920s, Peter was regularly written about in the *Door County Advocate.* Though the coverage was generally positive, the paper regularly remarked on his race. "He was repeatedly referenced as the only black man in Door County," said Tashjian. Far more prejudicially, "when he married Julia, he is referred to as a 'darkie' in the paper. So, it's a complicated picture."

"He received community support, but then, there were racist things that routinely happened," she said.

Some of those incidents were subtle and some not so subtle. In the 1920s, the Ku Klux Klan was active in the state, including the Fox River Valley

Offers Prizes to Farmers for Grain Sheaves at Show

Special Bulletin Shows How to Prepare Samples

QUARTETTE SINGS AT FORESTVILLE TUESDAY EVENING

Only 7 More Days of this Great Sale

July Clearance

366 Pieces of High Grade Aluminum Ware

Including Percolators, Roasters, Fry Pans, Double Boilers, Preserve Kettles, and many other wanted articles. Values to $2.00. Your choice of the lot for Saturday and Monday only 88c

Exceptional July Clearance Value

52 Tailored Waists

Ladies, here's good news for you. Dainty Waists in plain white and some colors, pretty embroidered trimmings; values to $2.98. On sale starting Saturday until the lot is sold— 98c

Exceptional July Clearance Value

One Lot of Women's Dresses Values to $15.00

$6.98

The July Clearance Sale Continues in Our Grocery Dept.

THE FAIR STORE "Sturgeon Bay's Underprice Store"

KU KLUX KLAN BIG RALLY!

AT

Sturgeon Bay, Wisconsin

Sunday, July 26th, 1925

Ku Klux Klan, Juniors
American Krusaders
and Women of the Klan
Provincial Klonvocation
Public Naturalization
Krack Drill Team
National Public Speakers
Something Doing all Day

Sawyer Old School Grounds; Speaking Begins 9:30

HOTEL NORTHLAND
Green Bay
Wisconsin
250 GUEST ROOMS
FIREPROOF
Sleep in Safety

CONSTIPATION
CHAMBERLAIN'S TABLETS

Above: Peter Custis's daughter Hannah. *Courtesy of Door County Historical Museum.*

Left: The KKK planned a rally in Sturgeon Bay in 1925 and took out an advertisement in the *Door County Advocate*, July 24, 1925. *Courtesy of Door County Library Newspaper Archives.*

area—and its reach had a foothold in Door County. In 1924, a cross was burned on the Sawyer (west) side of Sturgeon Bay—where Peter lived. And in 1925, the KKK erected and burned a large cross on Dunlap reef, in the middle of the bay.

"That participants were not alone satisfied with the burning cross to attract attention, but several heavy charges of dynamite or other explosives were discharged on the rocky reef. The charge was so heavy that buildings shook on both sides of the bay," the *Door County Advocate* reported after the incident.

"At the time, Peter worked as a street cleaner," said Tashjian. "Because of his job, he had to clean it [the burned cross] up."

"Street cleaner" was only one of the hats Peter Custis wore. During his life, he worked on steamships on Lake Michigan, was a baggage transfer assistant, worked at the Hagen and English quarry, was a night watchman at the Ellenbecker Factory in town, had a job of turning on the lights on the west side of Sturgeon Bay, was hired to paint the Sawyer firehouse, shoveled snow, broke up ice and was in charge of the Sawyer boathouse for a time.

"When he turned eighty-three, he was still employed," Tashjian said. Indeed, the paper reported his passing birthdays, remarking that Custis could still put in a full day's work.

Peter Custis's trash barrel wagon is featured at the Door County Historical Museum in Sturgeon Bay. *Courtesy of Heidi Hodges.*

Peter Custis's headstone at Bayside Cemetery in Sturgeon Bay. *Courtesy of Heidi Hodges.*

Custis was a resident of the city for over fifty years. He retired at the age of eighty-six in 1928 and turned his property over to the city in exchange for his care and funeral expenses.

In 1932, Peter died, most likely stricken by the flu. (The *Advocate* reported his death was due to the "disease in the city.") His funeral was held at the Friends church in town, and he was buried at Bayside Cemetery.

But the city reneged on its burial agreement, and Peter Custis was laid in an unmarked grave at Bayside Cemetery.

Years later, historians and friends placed a stone to mark his resting site.

Elizabeth Dreutzer Leads the Suffragettes

In the early 1900s, the wives and mothers, sisters and daughters, teachers, homemakers, churchgoers and women's club members of Sturgeon Bay were adept at managing their households, disciplining their children and having supper ready for their hungry families.

These women, as it turns out, were also empowered to fight for equal rights.

Although they worked hard at home—and some were employed outside the home—and were a vital part of their communities, women didn't have a voice in deciding who would serve as their district attorneys, city council members, senators, governors or presidents.

The suffragettes of Sturgeon Bay never became celebrated or famous. The content of their debates and speeches did not make it into the local papers. Yet like the national leaders of the woman's suffrage movement—Susan B. Anthony and Elizabeth Cady Stanton—these women helped propel the suffrage movement forward.

Mrs. Y.V. Dreutzer (née Elizabeth Hanson) helped lead the local suffrage charge. In 1882, this daughter of Swedish immigrants married a son of Swedish immigrants—Yngve Viking Dreutzer. Along with her husband, a prominent attorney and district attorney for Door County, she owned and operated Shoreside, a resort made up of several cottages near their farm, where they raised three children: Genevieve, Cedric and Carl.

So Dreutzer was already an extremely busy woman when she became involved in the suffrage movement. In 1887, a few years after Wisconsin voters ratified a referendum giving women the right to vote

Elizabeth Dreutzer as a young woman. *Courtesy of Door County Historical Museum.*

at any election "pertaining to school matters," a group of Sturgeon Bay women—including Dreutzer—met to discuss the extent of their rights under this new referendum. As reported by the *Door County Advocate*, the group assigned a committee of three, "Mrs. Stokes, Mrs. Smith, and Mrs. Nelson," to do research.

These three representatives met with the city attorney, Dreutzer's husband, to clarify the "correct interpretation' of the amendment. Y.V. Dreutzer's opinion was that the amendment allowed any eligible woman "to vote at the charter election for mayor, alderman, treasurer, clerk, school commissioner, and assessor."

To facilitate voting at the next election, the paper reported that the women made arrangements to meet and "go in company to the polls" and invited a number of gentlemen to accompany them.

Consulting with an attorney in interpreting the law and visiting the polls en masse with men in tow were not just good ideas—they were necessary. Anti-suffrage sentiment was common, and this law was general enough to be open to interpretation.

This proved to be the case in Racine County in 1887. Wisconsin Women's Suffrage Association (WWSA) leader Olympia Brown's ballot in the spring election had been rejected because, in addition to voting for the school board, she also cast a vote for municipal candidates, whose offices also pertained to school matters (the very issue which Y.V. Dreutzer deemed legal in Sturgeon Bay). Brown later brought suit; the circuit court ruled in her favor, but the decision was later overturned by the state supreme court. The court ruled that in future elections, school board candidates should have a separate ballot (so that women could not vote for any other positions.) But the Wisconsin legislature later refused to give the local governments power to create a separate ballot—in effect, abolishing women's right to vote on anything involving school matters (https://www.wisconsinhistory.org/turningpoints/tp-032).

Therefore, it was quite probable that the Sturgeon Bay women might encounter resistance when they showed up at the polls to place their votes for candidates who made decisions regarding school matters and needed the support of like-minded men.

While Elizabeth Dreutzer had the support of her husband in the fight for equal rights, not every man (or woman) was so enlightened. Many felt that granting women the right to vote would lead to the destruction of the family.

Judge William H. Timlin, a Wisconsin Supreme Court judge with ties to both Door and Kewaunee Counties, was quoted in the *Advocate* in 1912 as saying that giving women the right to vote would "promote discord and weaken family ties," leading women to learn the "low practices and dirty deceits of politics." Judge Timlin maintained that suffrage would encourage women to be disloyal to their husbands and neglect the needs of their children. He concluded that there was "no good reason" for woman's suffrage; in fact, "some few" women even wanted it, and the country already had too many "ignorant" voters as it was.

Not to be deterred by the anti-suffrage movement, Dreutzer and her fellow suffragettes continued their campaign. In April 1912, a group of women met with Olympia Brown to form the Sturgeon Bay Women's Suffrage League, and seventy women joined the organization on the spot. Mrs. Emily Norden, Mrs. Jessie Blakefield, Mrs. Mary Mullen, Mrs. Edward Reynolds, Mrs. A.H. Stiles and Mrs. J. Rosenberg took on leadership roles in the Sturgeon Bay organization. Dreutzer herself was voted chairperson of the Door County Woman's Suffrage League.

It wasn't long before Dreutzer had organized a series of debates and lecture tours for the entire county. Recruiting suffrage speakers—attorneys Frank and Catherine Waugh McCulloch from Chicago and Harriet E. Grim from New York City—Dreutzer arranged for an automobile lecture tour throughout Door County from June 26 to July 3.

The stop in Sturgeon Bay on June 26, 1912, drew a crowd of five hundred people, according to the *Door County Democrat*. The large crowd stood in front of the Hotel Waldo (razed in 1967, it is today the site of Associated Bank on Third Avenue) and listened as the speakers lectured from the car. Dreutzer accompanied the tour as it made stops throughout Door County—Valmy, Jacksonport, Baileys Harbor, Fish Creek, Sister Bay, Ephraim, Egg Harbor, Maplewood, Forestville and Brussels—distributing leaflets and raising funds for the cause.

Elizabeth Dreutzer later in life. *Courtesy of Door County Historical Museum.*

Dreutzer, who was widowed in 1907 at the age of forty-seven, continued to encourage women voters even after the Nineteenth Amendment to the U.S. Constitution, granting women the right to vote, was finally ratified in 1920. That same year, she helped organize the Republican Women's Club—a precursor to the League of Women Voters—in Sturgeon Bay, of which she was named chairperson.

By the time she died in 1954 at the age of ninety-four, Elizabeth Dreutzer was living in Cincinnati with her daughter, but her roots were deeply rooted in Sturgeon Bay. She remained a charter member of the Sturgeon Bay Women's Club and spent every summer with her son and family at her old homestead on the bay shore of Sturgeon Bay.

PART II

Tragedies

A Pain that Can't Be Spoken

A Blaze in the Night Destroys the Heart of Sturgeon Bay

"Twelve Buildings Go Up in Smoke" was the *Door County Advocate* headline on November 4, 1880.

It was a conflagration that set the stage for a complete remodeling of Sturgeon Bay.

The fire, of undetermined causes, was spotted in the middle of the night. According to the *Advocate* story, "A bright light across the street, at about half-past three o'clock on Tuesday morning, caused Louis Colard to rush from his tailor-shop with cries of 'Fire!' A glance showed him that a lively flame was glowing in the harness-shop of Isadore Buschonville."

A fire was starting to kindle on Cedar Street—what is now Third Avenue in downtown Sturgeon Bay. Colard rushed through town, rousing the slumbering inhabitants and trying to muster up firefighting help. But rounding up help proved harder than expected, "probably because most of our citizens were engaged until a late hour on the previous evening in preparing for election day," the *Advocate* reported:

> *Much valuable time was lost in securing enough hands to man the fire engine, but a still more serious delay occurred in the effort to obtain a supply of water from the public well on the corner of Cedar and Spruce streets.... It was not until at least half an hour of precious time had elapsed that the discovery was made that there was not water enough in the well to keep the engine at work five minutes and that what little there was of the fluid was beyond the reach of the suction pipe. The bay was the only resource, and to this, the engine was removed.*

Every moment that passed allowed the fire to ravage the "light wooden buildings." The firemen soon encountered a new problem—the hose they had wasn't long enough to reach the far end of the fire. "Five hundred feet of hose is too little to be of much service, if the water supply must be obtained from the bay. If there had been two or three hundred feet more, there is no doubt that the fire could have been kept within small compass. It certainly could not have crossed the street, and Village Hall could have been easily saved."

The delays in response and the lack of both water and hose were lamented by townspeople. "From Louis Colard's description of the fire, as he first saw it, a few buckets of water would have put it out. Unluckily, there was no water, no buckets, and no one out of bed to carry them."

The *Advocate* reported heroic—or perhaps foolhardy—acts that may have prevented the fire from claiming even more buildings in the burgeoning town:

> *One of the most conspicuous figures of the night was James Madden. To his courage and heroism we are indebted for the saving of much valuable property....he was exposed to a heat so fierce that his clothing was burned. Several times did those who were assisting him ask him to relinquish a useless struggle, but his only answer was, "Come back boys, we will save it yet!" And they did save it. If not for James Madden, the* [Northwestern] *hotel, Lawrence & Co's store, and probably every building on that side of Cedar Street would have been destroyed.*

Consider this description from the *Advocate* of two men trying to save another structure: "One of the men hung over the edge of the building, head downward, while his companions grasped his legs, and in this dangerous position was able to throw water where it would do the most good."

With tongue in cheek, the *Advocate* added: "As far as we can learn, neither of these men ever traveled with a circus."

For all the heroism, there were plenty of gawkers and some who tried to help but only made matters worse. And there was at least one conspicuous act of opportunism:

> *This was rather hard on those who volunteered to run the machine, as they were forced to continue at their exhausting work long after they were really fit to do so. It was observed, however, that those who took the greatest pains to avoid being of any service were promptly on hand when John Graass's*

> *liquor-cellar was emptied upon the street, and heroically manned any kind of a vessel that would hold a drink of whiskey.*

But there was a bright spot. The night was calm—the first time in weeks—perhaps helping to spare some outlying structures.

Nevertheless, in little more than two hours, twelve buildings—comprising the heart of Sturgeon Bay at the time—were reduced to smoldering ruins, according to the *Advocate*: "In that brief period disappeared the accumulations of years of toil and frugality, together with pleasant homes and a thousand articles grown dear through association, and which money can never replace."

According to the *Advocate*, money wasn't even going to replace the buildings. Insurance companies were expected to foot the bill for only half of the damages, estimated to be $20,000—well over $250,000 in today's dollar.

Among the losses were the Village Hall, Graass's Saloon, the telegraph station, a tailor shop, the harness business and several homes. Some vowed to rebuild, but because it was so late in the season, many of those plans would have to wait until spring. Graass, probably to the relief of many in town, immediately began to contract for reconstruction of his saloon.

Looking north along Third Avenue in downtown Sturgeon Bay, mid-1940s. *Courtesy of Door County Historical Museum.*

Looking north along Cedar Street (now Third Avenue) in downtown Sturgeon Bay, in the early 1900s. *Courtesy of Door County Historical Museum.*

But for the rest of the town, it was decision time. It had been nine years since the devastating Peshtigo Fire, which occurred at the same time as the Great Chicago Fire. That fire jumped across the bay of Green Bay and devastated the southern portion of Door County, but it largely spared Sturgeon Bay.

With the lingering memory of that fire in 1871 and the exceedingly fresh memory of this one in 1880, those who vowed to rebuild had to consider using brick and mortar.

And so, the second version of Sturgeon Bay began, one that is still evident today, on its historic Third Avenue—the heart of Sturgeon Bay.

A Wave of Death

The Sinking of the Hackley

By all accounts, October 3, 1903, was a normal early autumn day. There was a strong wind blowing from the south, but that wasn't unusual.

It had been blowing earlier in the day when the *Erie L. Hackley*, a seventy-nine-foot steamer built in 1882, departed Sturgeon Bay, en route to Menominee, Michigan, on the other side of Green Bay.

It was an important and new route, bringing passengers and freight back and forth from the mainland of Wisconsin and the Upper Peninsula of Michigan to the Door Peninsula. The *Hackley* was the first ship procured for the newly formed Fish Creek Transportation Company. Four men—Joseph Vorous, E.T. Thorp, Orin Rowin and Henry Robertoy—purchased the steamer for $3,000.

The route was a great convenience for folks, who could make the passage in an hour or so. On land, the trip was one hundred miles or more, without developed roads, depending on the destination.

The day wasn't over for the *Hackley* after it arrived in Menominee. The old steamer loaded back up with nineteen passengers and cargo, bound for Egg Harbor, north of Sturgeon Bay, with more stops farther north along the peninsula.

The steamer departed Menominee at 5:00 p.m.

The weather did not improve. It was so questionable, in fact, that some passengers loaded their cargo but decided against boarding the ship themselves. It was, it turned out, the right decision. "Although blowing hard from the south and a big sea running, the steamer made good weather of it from Menominee to Green Island," the *Door County Democrat* reported that week.

The *Hackley* held its own, despite "laboring hard in the big sea." About an hour into the voyage, while the *Hackley* was in the middle of the bay, in the lee of Green Island, a violent squall sprang up.

Then, as the ship left the sheltering safety of the island, the vessel was hit with even stronger winds than it had been battling. A heavy downpour commenced. "The wind which came, with the velocity of a cyclone, struck the steamer broadside, and threw her down until the force of the water broke in the gangways, and the water rushed into the steamer."

Captain Joseph Vorous tried to get the ship turned into the wind, to "bring her head into it." But the powerful storm—possibly a tornado—had "blown the steamer over so far that it was impossible to bring her head into it, and she laid over on her side and filled rapidly, it being only a few minutes from the time the squall struck her until she foundered and sank," reported the *Advocate*.

It was cold, dark and raining hard, with terrific gale-force winds.

The ship's purser, F.C. Blakefield, described the scene, as reported by the *Democrat*: "I was in the pilot house but a few minutes when I felt her sinking and Capt. Vorous and myself knew it was not safe to remain there any longer. I jumped out onto the deck and ran aft along the windward side. I did not see the captain again, and he must have got caught in some of the wreckage and carried down with the steamer."

Blakefield threw a settee overboard and jumped after it. After a time in the dark, churning waters, Blakefield found another piece of wreckage, holding three other people, floating by. "This piece of wreckage being the upper deck, the lifeboat was lashed to it. And in the boat were [three others]. A monster wave swept the boat from its lashings and threw the occupants into the water, but they were assisted back onto the raft by the others."

After a bit, the floating wreckage began to come apart, and Blakefield worked on gathering it together as best he could. But the survivors became separated. They were tossed about in the storm until 8:00 a.m. the following morning, when another steamer, the *Sheboygan*, spotted survivors on the main floating wreckage.

Blakefield, who had been separated from the main group, was spotted a mile and a half from shore, near Fish Creek. Others were farther out.

The ship's engineer, Orin Rowin, floated to a shoal near Chambers Island. "When rescued, life was nearly extinct, but it is thought that he will recover," the *Advocate* reported in the October 5, 1903 issue.

In all, the survivors had been exposed to frigid waters for over fourteen hours. Incredibly, of the people who clung to the wreckage, only one, George LeClair, was washed off and perished. The rest managed to persevere until morning. The others were not as lucky. Of the nineteen aboard, eleven died, in what turned out to be one of the worst maritime disasters in local history.

The body of passenger Freeman Thorp was found near Hat Island, in the middle of the bay just north of Egg Harbor. "He evidently had died from exposure, as he was lying across a plank, his coat sleeves being caught on a nail which held him to the wreckage."

And two sisters, Ethel and Edna Vincent, died together, although there were at least two different accounts of how they perished. "The last seen of the two Vincent girls was just before the steamer went down, when they threw their arms about each other and the supposition is that they fainted in the cabin," the *Democrat* reported.

Another report indicated they leaped into the water, hand in hand.

The *Advocate* reported that the girls were "lying in a dead faint. They were subsequently swallowed up by the ruthless maws of the insatiable sea. The eldest had been teaching in one of the public schools at Marinette and her sister was visiting her, the twain being on their way home."

Blakefield also recounted, to the *Advocate*, how another woman was lost:

> *The Barringer girl was pulled through the cabin door by Fireman McSweeney, assisted by the girl's brother Lawrence. McSweeney had hold of the Barringer girl's hand when they went into the water over the side of the sinking steamer, and in going down, their hold was broken and McSweeney came up first.*
>
> *As soon as he rose to the surface he struck out for the yawl boat which was close to him, and pulling himself into it, endeavored to reach the Barringer girl, who was then struggling in the water nearby. While McSweeney was attempting the girl's rescue, the yawl was swamped and he was thrown into the water, and at about the same time, the Barringer girl went down for the last time. McSweeney then struck out for the upper works, on which he saved himself.*
>
> *Nothing was seen of Lawrence Barringer after he struck the water, but as he was an excellent swimmer and a brave lad, he undoubtedly lost his life in trying to save his sister.*

There were reports of close calls—such as the folks who didn't board the ship in the first place. For example, the Reimers family was moving to Egg Harbor and decided against boarding at the last minute. Ed Thorp of Fish

Creek, one of the owners of the *Hackley*, also intended to return home on the steamer but changed his mind because of the weather.

And there was one dramatic front-page report in the October 17, 1903 issue of the *Advocate* of how the disaster was foretold in a dream.

> *The warning came to Roy Thorp* [his brother Ed was one of the *Hackley*'s owners, and brother Freeman died of exposure] *during Friday night. He dreamt he saw the* Hackley *battling with a terrible storm on Green bay and there go down. The vision that came in the dead of night portrayed the passengers rushing about frantic with fear and fervently praying for their lives. Suddenly the little steamer gave a lurch and dove beneath the surface. Passengers and crew were thrown into the water and one by one were seen to give up and sink beneath the surface.*

The dream caused Thorp to wake at 3:00 a.m. "He dressed himself and read the papers but could not get the matter out of his mind." He considered contacting his brother, Freeman Thorp, in Menominee but changed his mind, "thinking it foolish to permit a dream to cause him any alarm....[B]ut on Sunday morning when the terrible news came over the wire, his dream came back and he regretted that he did not send word as he intended."

His brother Freeman Thorp was one of the eleven found dead.

As soon as the word of the disaster spread, help mobilized.

The Canal Life-Saving Station (today a Coast Guard station) responded, "arriving in the vicinity of the shipwreck, the tug and crew patrolled the course from there to Fish Creek in hopes of discovering more wreckage and rescuing more of the shipwrecked persons," wrote the *Advocate* in the October 5, 1903 issue. "At Fish Creek this morning, the life-saving crew darted for Green Island to drag for the missing persons, having with them a member of the crew of the *Hackley* to point out just where the accident occurred."

By the end of the month, four victims were recovered, including the Vincent sisters, who were found at the bottom, only three feet apart.

As soon as word was out about the disaster, folks began to debate and argue causes and fault. "It is an outrage for the companies who have no excuse for doing so to send their old hulks out in the lake and bay when they should have long since been condemned by the government inspectors" wrote the *Advocate*. "These old hulks are sent out to carry your friends and mine. I say, gentleman, it is an outrage, and I hope that the terrible fate of the *Hackley* will awaken with people to the danger that menaces them and theirs whenever they set foot on one of these crazy boats."

Shortly after the tragedy, the *Advocate* recounted a conversation between some experienced captains. "Capt. Johnson said that he had never considered the *Hackley* a perfectly safe boat," the paper reported. "She always seemed to be top heavy…the mistake made was in trying to head her into the sea instead of running before the gale, which could have been done if her steering gear was in order. If, however, this was out of repair, there was no help for the unfortunate craft, no matter what those on board could have done or did do."

The *Advocate* also asserted,

> *The fate of the steamer* Hackley *has unquestionably sealed the doom of using small steamers as a means of transportation on Green Bay. It will be a long time before the public will be able to drive from their memory the terrible calamity, and just so long as the disaster is remembered, there will be a feeling of fear and timidity in the public mind against traveling on this class of steamers.*

A year later, the debate still raged, and even the inspectors were scrutinized. The competing papers at the time, the *Democrat* and the *Advocate*, took different sides in the debate. The *Democrat* took the *Advocate* to task for publishing a possibly disguised letter to the editor ridiculing the inspector general of steam vessels.

"The inspectors found that no boat of the *Hackley* class could have survived that storm," the *Democrat* argued, while calling the editor of the *Advocate* "mad" for disparaging the "brave and noble Capt. Vorous who died at his post trying to save his craft and the lives of its passengers."

Vorous's body was reportedly recovered on October 30, 1903, and buried in Blossomberg Cemetery in Fish Creek.

Shortly after the wreck, folks on the Door Peninsula, particularly north of Egg Harbor, found flotsam and jetsam from the *Hackley*, including wood from the ship and "a couple kegs of beer and some other freight" on the beach in Sister Bay. A couple weeks later, the wreck itself was discovered, but the depth prevented any serious investigation.

After those recovery efforts, the *Hackley* was left unexplored for almost eight decades, until late 1981, when diver Frank Hoffman rediscovered the remains in 110 feet of water, two miles northeast of Green Island.

Hoffman was known for raising the "Mystery Ship," the intact schooner *Alvin Clark*, from the bottom of the bay near Chambers Island. Hoffman and his crew of divers made an attempt to raise the *Hackley* from the depths, too, but failed.

In 1987, his divers returned to the *Hackley* and, without authorization, removed bones of two people. Those two unidentified victims were interred at Bayview Cemetery in Sturgeon Bay.

Today, *Hackley* still rests on the bottom of the dark, murky bay, a testament to the dangers of maritime travel and a memorial to those who perished on that fateful October night in 1903.

Horror at the Harris Home

The sun had gone down for the night on Monday, June 29, 1953. *Advocate* editor Sumner Harris told his wife, Grace, he would be staying late at the office to write up a review of a special movie that was at the Door Theater: *House of Wax*.

The movie was a big deal in town. Running for only four days at the Door Theater in Sturgeon Bay, it was the first 3D feature produced by a major studio. The horror film stars Vincent Price as a wax museum owner who murders people to repopulate his fire-damaged wax museum.

The Door Theater took out a quarter-page advertisement in the paper, with eye-catching graphics and provocative slogans: "Nothing on the screen you've ever heard about or seen can compare with the astounding sensation Warner Bros. brings you now in natural vision: 3 Dimension!"

"It comes right at you!"

"Man-turns-monster gripping a city in panic!"

Sumner was excited to see the movie. He talked with his fellow *Advocate* employees, who later recalled him telling the staff, "I told my wife I was going to see that movie if I had to work until midnight."

Grace Harris, perhaps not interested in a horror flick, stayed home at their residence on Michigan Street while her husband went to the 6:50 p.m. screening. He first stopped by their son Chandler's residence to drop off some correspondence to edit.

When the movie ended, Sumner returned to the office a little after 9:00 p.m., called Chandler to tell him about the film and began writing his review.

Above: A youthful Chandler Harris with his parents, Grace and Sumner, circa 1936. *Courtesy of Kathy Anschutz.*

Left: Sumner Harris at his *Door County Advocate* office desk. *Courtesy of Door County Historical Museum.*

THURSDAY, JUNE 25, 1953 — DOOR COUNTY ADVOCATE, STURGEON BAY, WISCONSIN — SECTION 1—PAGE FIVE

In and Out of Town

The Advocate welcomes news from its readers for this column, as well as all other news items. If you take a trip or have visitors from out-of-town, we'll appreciate your calling us. Just phone 1100.

"Miss Door County" Entry Blank

Name

Address

Age (not less than 18 nor over 28 Sept. 1, 1953)

Parents' Name and Address

School Attended

If graduated, when

Mail this to DOOR COUNTY CHAMBER OF COMMERCE Sturgeon Bay, Wis.

West Side

Washington Is.

Clyde McCoy's Band Slates Appearance

WANTED — BARTENDER. Write A. C., c/o Advocate.

at John Draeb's

NEW

Heritage

Magnificent new pattern of timeless beauty

1847 ROGERS BROS.

The first and only silverplate to bring you the rich traditional Victorian design you've admired in sterling.

SEE IT ON YOUR TABLE TONIGHT!

JOHN J. DRAEB Jewelry Gifts

SKYWAY DRIVE-IN Theatre

Between Fish Creek and Ephraim

2 Shows Nightly—1st Show at Dusk—Doors Open 7 p.m.

Fri.-Sat. DOUBLE FEATURE June 26-27

IN TECHNICOLOR

"Jack McCall, Desperado"

With GEORGE MONTGOMERY — ANGELA STEVENS

2ND FEATURE

"African Treasure"

Sun.-Mon. June 28-29

ABBOTT and COSTELLO MEET CAPTAIN KIDD

ALSO "NO PETS ALLOWED" — "BEEP BEEP" "DAREDEVIL DAYS" — LATEST NEWS

Tues.-Wed.-Thurs. June 30-July 1-2

CALL IT LOVE...

CLASH BY NIGHT

Join "EGGIE" and "GREGGIE" "DOWN ON THE FARM"

Tues. - Thurs. - Sat. 6:15 - 7:00 A.M.

WOKW

1050 ON THE DIAL

DOOR THEATRE

4 DAYS STARTING SUNDAY

SUNDAY CONTINUOUS FROM 1:30

EVENINGS AT 6:50 AND 9:00

Entertainment has never known its equal!

FIRST FEATURE PRODUCED BY A MAJOR STUDIO IN 3D!

NOTHING ON THE SCREEN YOU'VE EVER HEARD ABOUT OR SEEN CAN COMPARE WITH THE ASTOUNDING SENSATION WARNER BROS. BRING YOU NOW IN NATURAL VISION

3 DIMENSION

IT COMES RIGHT AT YOU!

Man-turned-Monster gripping a city with panic, craving the show-world's beauties for his Chamber of Horrors!

HOUSE OF WAX

WARNERCOLOR

VINCENT PRICE · FRANK LOVEJOY · PHYLLIS KIRK

PLUS — CARTOON — NEWS

Scofield Company

A GOOD HARDWARE STORE

We have added to our line of fine major appliances the well known and accepted Westinghouse merchandise. This new line includes the famous frost-free two door refrigerators. It is the world's first completely automatic frost free two door. There is no defrosting to do in the big freezer or the spacious refrigerator with completely automatic temperature control to keep all foods better than ever. Westinghouse Speed electric range with the automatic corox with electronic eye—America's favorite laundry twins—the Westinghouse Laundromat and Electric Clothes Dryer—Westinghouse certified water heater and many other Westinghouse appliances. These super-performers all yours on inviting easy time payments.

It's the song ye sing and the smile ye wear That's making the sun shine everywhere.

DOOR THEATRE

FRIDAY AND SATURDAY

DOUBLE FEATURE

SAFARI DRUMS

REX ALLEN SOUTH PACIFIC TRAIL

SATURDAY MATINEE ONLY — 2:40 - 3:15 ELEVENTH CHAPTER OF "RADAR MEN"

DONNA THEATRE NOW Thru Saturday

THE LOVE STORY OF A PRINCESS!

YOUNG BESS

SIMMONS · GRANGER · KERR · LAUGHTON

AND REX THOMPSON

ADDED — IN THE NEWS — COMMUNIST RIOTS IN EAST GERMANY

SUNDAY—MONDAY—TUESDAY

SUNDAY MATINEE AT 2:00 EVENINGS AT 7:00 AND 9:00

THE SAND-EATIN', BATTLE-BUSTIN' GUYS WHO STOPPED ROMMEL, THE DESERT FOX!

THE DESERT RATS

JAMES MASON · ROBERT NEWTON · RICHARD BURTON

AND—JOE McDOAKES COMEDY—CARTOON—NEWS

Door County Advocate

House of Wax advertisement in the June 25, 1953 *Door County Advocate. Courtesy of Door County Library Newspaper Archives.*

But then, something happened.

Sumner was spotted racing out of the alley behind the *Advocate*, heading in the direction of his home. Jack Schaefer, an announcer on the radio station WOKW and one of Sumner's business acquaintances, spotted the newspaper editor hastily driving away.

It was the last time anyone saw Sumner Harris alive.

The details of what happened next are still a bit foggy, but the overall picture was very clear.

Both Grace and Sumner were brutally murdered in their home.

The following morning, police received a call from Mark Duranty, a Harris neighbor. "My son has killed Mr. and Mrs. Harris," he reportedly announced to the chief of police, Romain Londo.

Duranty found a note on his fourteen-year-old son Jimmy's dresser. Its chilling message read, "Dear Mom, I killed Mr. and Mrs. H. You can call the police and tell them I'm in Michigan, because that is where I headed."

Sturgeon Bay's Assistant Chief of Police Wendell Warwick was immediately dispatched to the Harris house. Sumner's son Chandler, who was already at the *Advocate* office working on the edition due to be published that day, was also notified by Londo.

Chandler dropped everything and was second on the scene, followed by James Robertson, another *Advocate* reporter.

The scene was gruesome and shocking, especially for a sleepy, idyllic hamlet like Sturgeon Bay.

"Blood was spattered on the furniture and on the floor," the *Advocate* reported in its June 30 edition, printed only hours after the discovery of the murdered editor. "Signs of a struggle were in evidence....[A] package of Mr. Harris' brand of cigarettes lay nearby."

A *Door County Magazine* article written by Jeffrey Davis, who was able to interview Robertson, describes what happened at the crime scene.

> *Despite the severity of the crime, and the evidence gathering occurring, Robertson was allowed inside. His detailed account left the community in shock. He walked into the house, and "There were people walking everywhere. I'll never forget it," he said. The police seemed stunned, people were handling the murder weapon, and the* Advocate *photographer finally told the police to seal off the crime scene.*

Grace Harris's body, "clad only in undergarments," was found in the home, just off the living room. Sumner's body was nearby.

While the shocked and grieving *Advocate* reporters—including son Chandler—and staff churned out a newspaper, with the chilling account on the front page of the June 30, 1953 issue, police began searching for Jimmy Duranty. At first, efforts were focused on searching nearby Lake Michigan for signs of the Harris's car, which had gone missing. It was presumed Duranty had stolen the vehicle as well.

When searches nearby came up empty, the boy became the subject of a nationwide manhunt, newspapers across the country ran the shocking story and local police and clergy made appeals on the radio for the youth to return.

It was only the following day, Wednesday, July 1, when the fourteen-year-old was found in Shelbyville, Indiana, at 2:40 a.m., sleeping in the men's restroom of the Shelby County courthouse.

Duranty was arrested for vagrancy and claimed he was James Mead from Duluth, Minnesota. Authorities in Shelbyville discovered the Harrises' dark green 1949 Pontiac abandoned nearby. Seeing Wisconsin plates, the local sheriff remembered reading a story in the *Indianapolis Star* about the brutal double murder in Sturgeon Bay and connected the dots.

"When confronted by the sheriff and the evidence, Duranty still maintained his name was Mead. Then the sheriff showed the youth a suit coat taken from the car and it matched the pants the latter was wearing. The youth admitted he was James Duranty and that he had killed the Harrises."

He waived extradition to Sturgeon Bay. Door County sheriff Hallie Rowe, along with his son Harvey and Deputy Alex Meunier, left for Shelbyville on Wednesday night to bring the youth back. Duranty told authorities he didn't know why he committed the murders, saying, "I don't know why I did it, but I'm guilty. Something upstairs told me to do it."

The youth had attended St. Joseph's Catholic seminary at Westmont, Illinois, in anticipation of preparing for the priesthood. "He was a freshman at the school last year and had returned home about three weeks ago," the *Advocate* reported. "However, Mrs. Duranty said the school had informed her recently that her son had poor marks and was not eligible to return."

Duranty had often worked for Sumner Harris, cutting the lawn and doing odd jobs. "Mrs. Duranty said her son thought a lot of the Harrises."

According to the *Advocate*, Duranty said he "went to the Harris home about 7:30 Monday evening, knocking on the back door to gain entrance. He was admitted by Mrs. Harris and walked in. He said he tied and gagged Mrs. Harris, but that in about 20 minutes, she got free and tried to call police. Then, he inflicted the knife wounds, saying he believed she died almost instantly."

But he wasn't finished with his murderous spree.

"'I waited around the house for Sumner Harris to come home,' the youth said in his confession. 'He came in about 9:25 and he put up a fight, but he died almost instantly, too.'"

He continued in his detailed confession, which was reported in the *Advocate*:

> *After killing Mr. and Mrs. Harris, I went to my home, packed my clothing and again went to the Harris home, got their Pontiac automobile and took off.*
>
> *I went through Wisconsin and into Illinois and into Indianapolis, Ind. And then toward Shelbyville. About three miles northwest of there, I got onto a gravel road and when I attempted to turn around, I ran the automobile into the ditch. I left the car there and walked into Shelbyville.*
>
> *When I got into Shelbyville, I stopped at a gasoline station and then walked over by the bridge. A car stopped and a man started talking to me. He flashed a badge to me and informed me that I should not be out on the street as the state police could pick me up. He told me he would take me to the jail or courthouse and that I could sleep there.*
>
> *The man left and I came down to the courthouse and laid down in the restroom in the basement.*

That's where he was found and arrested.

Upon his return to Sturgeon Bay, the youth was met by over two hundred residents who gathered around the courthouse, waiting for hours for his return. Local officials radioed ahead, when the sheriff was in southern Door County, to let the returning officers know about the crowd. Duranty was whisked into a back door and into an upstairs cell.

Reports say he seemed to show no remorse, but another report suggested he "broke down upon seeing his parents."

After he was deemed sane and after scouring the state juvenile codes of the time, it was determined he could not be held past the age of twenty-one, despite the severity of the crime. And because of his young age, he could not be sent to a reformatory or prison.

Duranty was taken to the only facility available, the Waukesha School for Boys, on July 7, 1953, only one week after the murders.

"The young slayer of Mr. and Mrs. Sumner Harris faces a penalty of six years' imprisonment for his crime, not a life term that an adult murderer would receive in this state," a front page *Advocate* story reported.

The community was outraged—so much so, that District Attorney Herbert Johnson and juvenile judge G.M. Stapleton issued a statement, published on the front page of the July 7, 1953 *Advocate*. They acknowledged that the community was shocked by the murder but that the law was clear. "Let us have confidence and courage in the wisdom of our laws and our legislators and in the disposition of the case thereunder," they wrote.

Certain questions remained. While Duranty confessed to stabbing Grace, an autopsy discovered she had actually died of strangulation, not the knife wounds that were later inflicted. And there was no explanation for finding her body clad only in her undergarments.

It was also never clear why Sumner left his office in such a hurry. The confessed killer didn't mention Grace trying to call Sumner. And telephone operators didn't remember patching such a call. It was theorized Sumner left the *Advocate* office in reaction to a frantic call made by Grace. Still, it was unclear why she would have called him and not the police, since she knew he was going to be at the movie.

Regardless of the details, the path ahead for the young Chandler Harris was clear. A recent college graduate, he was thrust into the position of editor and owner.

Indeed, Chandler worked as editor of the paper—one of the largest non-daily papers in the state and Midwest—until the late 1980s, when he sold it to newspaperman Frank Wood. But instead of retiring, Chandler continued as editor emeritus, working at the paper until he died of a sudden heart attack at his desk in 1998.

But the reality of the murders was still fresh when *Advocate* put out the July 2, 1953 issue. Chandler wrote a personal piece on the front page, a tribute to his parents and a message to the community:

> *Faith was their strength; faith in people and their essential nobility....*
>
> *Sum in particular held by people the rest of the community rejected as worthless. He was their worth, encouraged them and had the satisfaction of seeing human souls recreated by a little spark he had lent.*
>
> *He was so kind, we sometimes got angry and wished he could be more coldly practical. Sum wasn't built that way. His patience was infinite, his generosity unceasing. Gay had a quicker temper, but only because it hurt her to have him take any unjustified abuse. As the newspaper and community service were his life, he was hers. It is grimly fortunate she did not live a widow.*

Jim Robertson, Chan Harris and Doug Larson, reporters at the *Door County Advocate. Courtesy of Door County Historical Museum.*

Chandler ended his tribute by vowing to keep the *Advocate* the same newspaper it had been and to carry on. "The task is nearly impossible, but with God's help and the help of those who mourn, it will be done."

The staff wrote their own tributes on the same page. Using their beloved editor's and his wife's more familiar names, the staff simply stated, "So long, Sum. So long, Gay."

Leathem Smith

The Final Heroic Act of a Sturgeon Bay Legend

The evening of June 24, 1946, was growing late. A party had been going on for some time at the Leathem Smith Lodge in Sturgeon Bay, but revelers were growing restless, awaiting the return of the lodge's namesake—the evening's guest of honor—from a day of sailing.

After the Leathem Smith Lodge facility underwent a remodel, the evening was set as a celebration of the grand opening, just in time for summer tourist season.

Leathem Smith had spent many a day sailing with friends and family aboard his beloved sailing sloop the *Half Moon*—formerly owned by Jimmy Roosevelt, son of President Franklin D. Roosevelt—which Smith refitted to accommodate his ailing father, who suffered from the effects of polio.

This early summer day was no different, remembered Carl Raymond Christianson, a friend of Smith's, who had been asked to go along on the day's sail across the bay to the Marinette Yacht Club, where another party was happening.

Smith offered to bring other friends along for the ride. Christianson had other commitments, he wrote in his 1989 book *Shipbuilding and Boat Building in Sturgeon Bay*. But two employees of Smith's boat yard, Elton Washburn and Howard Hunt, were able to join him. Smith's daughter Patsy and her friend Mary Loomis also went along for the ride.

"They partied at the yacht club [in Marinette] until dark," wrote Christianson, "and then left under power for Sturgeon Bay."

THE LEGACY

Smith, president and general manager of the Smith Shipbuilding Company, was the head of one of the longest continuously operated shipbuilding companies in the city.

The story of the yard began many decades earlier when, in the 1870s, John Leathem and Tom Smith ventured to the county to seek their fortunes in lumbering. The two young men purchased waterfront property along the banks of Sturgeon Bay and opened a sawmill.

"It was one problem to produce lumber, and another problem to get it to the market," wrote Christianson. The partners formed the Leathem and Smith Towing and Wrecking Company Corporation.

This continued for several decades until 1910, when the partnership was dissolved and the lumber mill sold. John Leathem moved from Sturgeon Bay, leaving Tom Smith behind. Smith expanded his business to building barges and tugs and continued towing and wrecking operations.

Tom Smith died in 1914, leaving the business to his youngest son, Leathem, named for Tom's former business partner. Christianson remembered Leathem Smith as a hard worker, starting from the early days of Smith's youth. When Leathem was old enough to work on the water, his father would pay him five cents to round up lost logs floating on the bay and take them to the mill. His work ethic continued to his shipyard days.

The young Leathem Smith, a recent college graduate, was suddenly thrust into the business world. "By the time he got everything squared around, the United States' involvement in World War I was fast approaching," wrote Christianson.

Smith was able to secure government contracts to build ten wooden tugs, and the business grew. He also began distributing coal to area customers after receiving large shipments. The name changed to reflect the new direction. It was now the Leathem D. Smith Coal and Dock Company. The yard performed so well on the first contract, it was awarded another contract for ten more tugs.

After the war, the young Smith, who was an engineer by education, considered the problems of unloading cargo—particularly coal—from older, obsolete ships and barges. If a vessel could be refitted to "self unload," it would no longer be obsolete.

In the early 1920s, he eventually lit upon an idea, and after trial and error, it worked. "For the next fifteen or twenty years, no less than thirty of these idle Great Lakes freighters had the scraper-style self unloaders installed on

Leathem Smith. *Courtesy of Door County Historical Museum.*

them and put back into service," wrote Christianson. The ships hauled coal, stone, sand, cement "and, on a few occasions, even salt."

In his book, Christianson remembered talking with Leathem Smith about a time when Smith was offered a lucrative patent deal for the unloader. But Smith turned the deal down in order to continue the installation work in his own yard. "The workmen in Sturgeon Bay are expecting me to bring in work for the winter," Christianson remembered Smith saying.

When the Depression hit, Smith was forced to get creative with finances and mortgages to survive until 1934, when his previous contracts began paying up and new work began flowing in.

Slowly and steadily, new orders for ships came. And in 1940, the yard landed an order for ten large freighters. It meant expanding the yard and expanding the workforce from 300 to 1,500 employees. But that proved more difficult than expected. It was during the early days of World War II, and building material for expansion was difficult to come by.

"It must be remembered that during this period, the only materials you could get were those that were assigned for the war effort. No steel could be purchased and used for docks and buildings or other purposes," wrote Christianson, who was working with Leathem Smith at the time. Instead, the new docks were constructed of wood, and material was salvaged from derelict buildings in Milwaukee.

"Everything was saved that could be saved from the building, including a large quantity of brick and other materials, which were practically non-existent on the open market," wrote Christianson, who headed the expedition to Milwaukee to find material for the expansion.

Expanding the workforce was another matter. It meant finding housing for the new crew. An employee barracks was built, and many prefabricated homes were built as well—homes that still stand in Sturgeon Bay today.

Buses ran from nearby communities, bringing in workers from as far north as Gills Rock on the Door Peninsula and as far south as DePere, Wisconsin, near Green Bay.

It was during this time that the shipyard became part of the movement of women into jobs traditionally performed by men. The Rosie the Riveter era had begun.

Astonishingly, at its peak, the yard built a ship a week, with 5,600 workers, 750 of which were women. Another 800 subcontractors were also involved, and 400 out-of-state subcontractors made ship parts.

As it turned out, the *Aldon Gifford*, the first boat in Leathem Smith's yard to be built under the new government contract, also was one of the first to land on Normandy. Smith devised another invention, a shipping container to help carry goods around the world via ship. Today, Smith's invention is the industry standard.

During the war, Smith decided to run for the U.S. Senate and was frequently absent from his post, leaving Christianson to head the yard. At one point, Christianson wrote, he was asked by Smith's Senate campaign crew if the shipyard could come up with a publicity stunt to draw media attention to Smith's campaign. Christianson considered the idea and suggested they could launch two ships on the same day.

The campaign crew was enthused but asked if the yard could launch a staggering *four* ships in one day.

With changed schedules, movement of huge equipment and thirty-second windows in which to accomplish the launchings, it happened.

Despite the herculean effort by Christianson and the yard, Smith ultimately lost the election.

TRAGIC END

It was June 24, 1946. The partygoers at Leathem Smith Lodge were growing concerned as they waited for the sloop's arrival. It was unusual, as Smith had been looking forward to the grand reopening of his lodge. Christianson, who was in attendance, remembered the growing concern.

A call was made to the Marinette Yacht Club. They learned Smith had left much earlier in the day—and should have arrived in Sturgeon Bay. Soon, the Coast Guard was called—and the gathered friends hoped Smith had managed to get the *Half Moon* to an island in the middle of Green Bay to avoid a strong squall that had swept through.

But the search turned up nothing. The *Half Moon* and its passengers had disappeared.

About four o'clock the next morning, the fate of the *Half Moon* and passengers was finally learned. Smith's daughter Patsy was found along the shore north of Sturgeon Bay, alive. All of the others, including Leathem Smith, had drowned.

Patsy told the story to reporters who swarmed her when she was discovered. According to the *Door County Advocate*'s June 28, 1946 front-page story, Patsy explained that a sudden squall overcame the sloop:

> *She and Mary Loomis, who was her roommate at Pine Manor College at Wellesley, Mass., were in the small cabin resting when the squall struck, and rushed out into the cockpit. Her first thought was to loosen the jib—but it was torn to shreds before she could untie the rope, she said.... The breakers were sweeping right over the boat, she said, and it was impossible to head up. The cockpit quickly filled, and life-preservers kept there were swept away except for one which Patsy said Hunt retrieved*

> *after the boat had capsized and the occupants were momentarily clinging to the spar for support before the yacht completely filled and sank.*
>
> *Patsy credited her father with a noble act when she cited that he wrapped the lone life preserver around Mary and told the girls to try and make shore.*
>
> *"Dad winked at me and said, 'Patty, take care of mother.'"*

Christianson, who talked to Patsy personally, reported in his book that Patsy's friend Mary had almost made the long swim to shore. They had been together, sharing the one life preserver they had.

"Patsy's feet touched the rocky bottom of the shore, she turned and yelled to her companion, 'We've made it! We've made it! I'm on shore!' She crawled up on the rocky shore and when she looked for her girlfriend, the life preserver was empty," he wrote.

Leathem Smith tried to swim back toward Marinette. Howard Hunt could not swim and was last seen climbing the mast. "Elton Washburn, on the other hand, was an excellent swimmer and he followed the girls for maybe a mile or two before he disappeared from sight."

Patsy was discovered by Mr. and Mrs. Frank Hood along a normally unpopulated stretch of beach, north of the bay of Sturgeon Bay. "Mrs. Hood was a trained nurse and had her husband carry Patsy up to the beach house, put her in bed, and crawled in alongside of Patsy to try to warm her up." Soon, an ambulance arrived.

"When Dr. Dorchester arrived, he immediately called the Lodge to apprise the people of what had happened," Christianson remembered.

The likely cause of the sudden sinking was the hatch Smith had made in the bulkhead to accommodate his father's disability, Christianson wrote. It was a risk Smith was aware of, but he had dismissed the potential problem because he enjoyed the freedom the hatch afforded him.

The aftermath of Leathem's death was immediate. Insurance adjusters insisted that Smith's body be located, and it was, with Christianson leading the charge. In fact, all the bodies were discovered, save for Mary Loomis, within a few days. "This surely was one of the greatest dragging and recovery operations in marine history for all time," Christianson wrote.

The city and many different agencies, including a troop of young Boy Scouts, were called on to help find Loomis. Her body was eventually located by a fly fisherman later that week.

On the business side of the tragedy, stockholders of Leathem D. Smith Shipbuilding Corporation decided to close the yard and liquidate the equipment.

Leathem D. Smith's headstone at Bayside Cemetery in Sturgeon Bay. *Courtesy of Heidi Hodges.*

After that process, the stockholders started seeking a purchaser for the property. Christianson, who had been fully enmeshed in the shipbuilding industry, met the best offer and, ultimately, purchased the property.

The name selected for the new corporation was Christy Corporation. In 1968, the Manitowoc Company purchased Christy Corporation and the adjacent business, Sturgeon Bay Shipbuilding, and created Bay Shipbuilding Company. The large yard continues to operate to this day as Fincantieri. The company builds marine vessels and is host to a large number of Great Lakes freighters during the winter lay-up for repairs and maintenance.

Although Smith never returned from that tragic sailing trip to be guest of honor at the grand reopening of his lodge, his legacy lives on in Sturgeon Bay—through his many contributions to the shipbuilding industry and the lodge, which has changed hands many times since 1946. It still bears his name, the Lodge at Leathem Smith, in honor and tribute to him.

The *Lakeland*

Mystery at the Bottom of Lake Michigan

December 2, 1924, was a stormy night on Lake Michigan. Ships still plying the waters so late in the season scrambled to seek shelter. Autumn had drawn to a close, and the shipping season slowed, but the *Lakeland*, loaded with a crew of twenty-seven men and a cargo of twenty-two automobiles, was on a voyage from Chicago to Detroit.

To wait out the storm, *Lakeland* captain John McNeely brought the bulk freighter into the safety of the Sturgeon Bay Ship Canal's turning basin, just off shore. Early the next morning, the weather cleared, and the *Lakeland* departed again, moving out into open waters.

But the steam-driven propeller ship didn't resume its voyage. Two sailing vessels, the *Ann Arbor #6* and the *Cygnus*, came upon the *Lakeland* off shore and noticed the vessel "making turns, apparently looking for something," explained Tamara Thomsen, maritime archaeologist with Wisconsin Historical Society's Maritime Preservation and Archaeology program.

From 2013 to 2015, Thomsen did extensive research on the *Lakeland*—built in 1887 in Cleveland and originally named *Cambria*—as part of her work to get the vessel listed in the National Register of Historic Places.

Thomsen explained that the two sailing ships came alongside and offered assistance. The freighter was leaking, the *Lakeland* crew reported. And there wasn't enough power to run the pumps and the propeller.

One of the vessels offered to tow the ship back to Sturgeon Bay. Inexplicably, Captain McNeely refused the assistance, arguing the ship was

The *Lakeland* shipwreck rests in Lake Michigan, near the mouth of the Sturgeon Bay Ship Canal. *Courtesy of Tamara Thomsen, maritime archaeologist with Wisconsin Historical Society's Maritime Preservation and Archaeology program.*

too far gone to save. Then, against logic, the stricken ship dropped anchor in deep water, about six miles off shore from the canal.

"The other vessels were pleading with the captain to allow them to tow the *Lakeland* to shallow water. But the captain refused lines that were cast to him and refused to relinquish the vessel," said Thomsen.

Eventually, the *Lakeland* lowered life rafts, and most of the crew moved over to the *Ann Arbor #6*. "All but a few left....They even removed everyone's baggage. Still, the captain and chief engineer remained behind," said Thomsen.

They had plenty of time to abandon ship, as the sinking process took over three hours. At one point, hatch covers blew forty feet into the sky, as air pressure built up during the sinking.

The *Ann Arbor #6*'s young telegraph operator Elliot Jacobson had a camera on board. "He photographed the entirety of the sinking process," providing one of the first photographic records of a ship sinking in the Great Lakes.

As the drama played out, Captain McNeely eventually escaped to a lifeboat, keeping hold of a line attached to the *Lakeland*, not relinquishing command of the ship—and therefore, according to maritime law, remaining

The *Lakeland* slowly sinks off the Sturgeon Bay Ship Canal, photographed by Elliot Jacobson, a young telegraph operator aboard the *Ann Arbor #6*, the vessel that arrived to the rescue of the *Lakeland*'s crew. *Courtesy of the National Archives in Chicago.*

The anchored *Lakeland* slowly sinks. It was later determined the ship was intentionally scuttled with twenty-two automobiles on board. *Courtesy of the National Archives in Chicago.*

The *Lakeland*'s crew of twenty-seven was rescued, minus the captain, who waited until the last moment to abandon ship, ensuring he remained in control of the sinking vessel. *Courtesy of the National Archives in Chicago.*

The *Lakeland* sinks beneath the surface, settling two hundred feet below. *Courtesy of the National Archives in Chicago.*

in control as captain—as the 297-foot vessel disappeared under the waves to the bottom, 200 feet below. At the bottom, the ship settled on its stern and broke in two.

"Water depth off the ship canal is about sixty feet, for quite a distance out, then, it drops off to two hundred feet quickly—it's where everyone fishes now," said Thomsen. "They [the *Lakeland* crew] were searching for this depth to scuttle the vessel." It was an obvious conclusion: "People weren't able to dive that deep at that time—so, [it was assumed] there could be no recovery or investigation," said Thomsen.

"So, the ship sinks, everyone goes to Sturgeon Bay and a couple crew members make statements to the *Door County Advocate*," said Thomsen. "They [the crew] said that it's in too deep of water and cannot be salvaged. It was like they had rehearsed the statement. And that raised the hackles of the insurance companies."

INSURANCE INVESTIGATION LEADS TO GROUNDBREAKING RESEARCH

Since all indications pointed in the direction of an intentional sinking, the insurance companies, of course, wanted the wreck investigated.

"The underwriters shopped around for anyone who could dive to that depth," said Thomsen. And they found a company, Overseas Salvors out of New York, run by "Big Harry" Reinhardson.

Reinhardson was an ex–U.S. Navy diver, Thomsen explained. "He said, 'This dive could be done, but it would require the cooperation of the navy,'" she said. The navy, it turns out, was testing a method of deep diving using helium gas.

There were five navy divers stationed in Pittsburgh, Pennsylvania, where the U.S. Bureau of Mines had a research station. And they were keen on coming to Sturgeon Bay to dive on the shipwreck.

This initially puzzled Thomsen, who didn't understand why the navy was involved in the *Lakeland* investigation. "Why were navy divers in Sturgeon Bay, testing their dive tables on a commercial vessel? It didn't make sense to me," she said. "Then, digging into the layers of this stuff… and with a little bit of sleuthing, I found log books and letters between the divers and superiors, seeing if they could come to Wisconsin to do their [human] tests."

Although at first glance, the association between the Bureau of Mines, the navy, the *Lakeland* and helium appeared strange, there was a clear association. Helium was a strategic gas, Thomsen explained, a byproduct of mining. "The navy had sent their top guys over there [to Pittsburgh] to look at helium for diving. They were using guinea pigs to test it, then dogs. And they were at a point to do human testing."

"The navy divers wrote to their bosses to get permission to come here and test these new diving schedules and gasses," said Thomsen. "But the officers said, 'No way!' So, the divers devised this scheme—they could take a vacation, and on their vacation time, they could work for Salvors. Their gas engineer took a vacation, as well."

In August 1925, the *Door County Advocate*'s headlines announced that the U.S. Navy was conducting diving tests in the *Lakeland* investigation. "But there was a whole lot more behind this," said Thomsen, who researched the mysteries.

Unfortunately, it didn't go very well.

"While those early pioneers of deep diving were closing in on a means of allowing longer and deeper dives, their method was still flawed," said Thomsen. Every diver on the 1925 team investigating the wreck experienced the bends, or decompression sickness, a painful condition in which bubbles from dissolved gasses form in the blood stream or tissues.

"I found the log from the gas-blending guy—we now think they didn't bring enough helium, the way modern divers dive now," said Thomsen. "Modern divers remove nitrogen and replace it with helium, so you don't get narcosis." Narcosis is a phenomenon that occurs at depths, causing divers to experience a foggy mental state, much like how nitrous oxide works at the dentist office.

But the 1925 divers were using it as a "wash out" gas, explained Thomsen. "They would dive with [regular compressed] air, then, on the way back, during decompression, they would replace with helium. They had it backwards…but it was their first thinking on it."

Thomsen said she told this story to a professor from Duke University, a leading expert on decompression issues. "I told him, 'Bet you didn't know the first helium dive was here in Wisconsin.'" Not many experts did, in fact, because the navy lost its enthusiasm for helium gas dives after the mostly unsuccessful attempt on the *Lakeland*, she said.

Later, however, another Wisconsinite, Dr. Edgar End, a physiologist at Marquette University and an expert in hyperbaric medicine, devised new methods to dive with helium and new dive tables—charts to determine the time needed to safely ascend from a deep dive.

"After testing the new tables on himself, he assisted another diver, Max G. Nohl, in setting a new world's record for open water deep diving by descending to a depth of 420 feet in Lake Michigan in 1937," wrote Thomsen in her research paper.

For comparison, the limit for recreational diving is 130 feet deep.

As for the *Lakeland*, the dive crew also made important discoveries regarding the sinking—certain valves were opened to take on water, they claimed. The evidence was later presented, "in agonizing detail," Thomsen said, by the insurance companies' lawyers.

National Register of Historic Places

Almost ninety years later, armed with the accumulated knowledge of decades of research and better diving technology, Thomsen was able to personally dive on the wreck. "It's a unique experience," said Thomsen. "It's like diving in an auto showroom. It's really a special place, to go there to visit."

Renowned underwater videographers John Janzen and John Scoles, who worked with *National Geographic* and the History Channel, were on hand to document the wreck.

Thomsen arranged a two-week field project on the *Lakeland*. "The goal was to be there for one week," with bad-weather dates built in. The divers were instructed to "video as much as possible and in as much detail as possible. Not the beauty shots, but a catalog. [They were] to stick a camera in every room," she explained.

That two-week stretch turned out to have absolutely perfect weather every day, remembered Thomsen, affording the crew plenty of time to accomplish their goals and then some. "We had an hour on the bottom every day, with an hour and a half to return [to the surface, with decompression time]. We captured all this video—more than you'd want to see—of the *Lakeland*," she said, laughing. "We tried to make sure we had full coverage."

Later, Thomsen returned to do more research diving on the *Lakeland*, this time with a few volunteers trained on taking measurements and making observations to support their bid to have the wreck listed in the National Register of Historic Places.

"There were five divers in the water every day. We had to write up the site plan and write a description of what it looks like on the bottom," for the listing.

They also evaluated every car still on board.

"There's lots of misinformation about the cars," said Thomsen. And for good reason—a lot of the early news was speculative at best. Even the captain and crew had different accounts of the number of cars aboard.

There were lawsuits, after the investigation in the mid-1920s, some settled out of court, so the information about the *Lakeland*'s cargo wasn't readily available, Thomsen explained. What she discovered, after doing research and video surveying, is that twenty-two cars—Nash, Kissel and Rollin—were aboard when the ship went down.

"There are twenty-one there currently—one was salvaged in the '70s," said Thomsen. "But [the salvagers] made an error in lifting it and dragged it into the [underwater] wall. They basically ripped all the sheet metal off the car." The recovered car remnants, determined to be a Rollin, were taken to the dump shortly after being lifted from the water.

With all the videos, photos and measurements, the shipwreck was unanimously approved for the National Register of Historic Places.

Listing a shipwreck is not particularly unusual, said Thomsen. They are routinely added to the National Register of Historic Places list because, in 1987, Congress passed the Abandoned Shipwreck Act, giving states ownership of wrecks on their bottom lands and allowing the historic designation. Once listed, it is easier to enforce laws protecting shipwrecks from looting and damage.

Wisconsin has sixty-three shipwrecks in the National Register, said Thomsen, "with three more in the queue and a couple more sitting back. It's a pipeline. Every year, we evaluate three or four. Not every one is eligible. Some are more broken up."

Different factors determine if a wreck is eligible. With the *Lakeland*, its unique history was important. Besides its interesting story, including the intentional sinking and its cargo of automobiles, "the part it played in evolving diving technology is one of several things it was able to be listed for."

THE CARGO: UNRAVELING A MYSTERY

But a big part of the *Lakeland*'s allure and mystery is the cars aboard.

Tamara Thomsen knows shipwrecks. But cars? "I can't change my own oil," she said, laughing. "I may not be the best person to write up about cars. But, I found that *one* guy."

Thomsen contacted Jim Dworschack of Soldiers Grove, Wisconsin, a collector of Nash automobiles. "I called him and left this crazy message on his voice mail....I said 'I'm an underwater archaeologist.'"

He called back, she explained, but he was traveling from LaCrosse, Wisconsin, to Milwaukee at the time. Since he was passing through Madison, where Thomsen is located, he agreed to stop in and see if he could identify the *Lakeland*'s cars from pictures and video.

"He said he had a half hour. Well, four and a half hours later, he could not believe the cars. We went through all them."

Dworschack could identify the Nashes, built in Kenosha, Wisconsin. "He told me all this info about them and said they were 'the common man's automobile,'" said Thomsen.

With the Nashes identified, Thomsen went in search of Kissel experts. Thomsen found a grandson, Doug Kissel, still in Hartford, Wisconsin, where the autos were built.

"They have a beautiful museum in Hartford," said Thomsen. She met with Kissel club members and Doug Kissel. There were, it turns out, seven Kissels on board. "They were carrying one of each kind available at the time," said Thomsen.

"These were cars for the wealthy. They were probably trying to get to Detroit for the auto show," she surmised, because each Kissel was unique and outfitted. "Every one of them...one had a tool box mounted on the running board, one had a clip for golf clubs."

The remaining five cars were not Nash, said Dworschack. And the Kissel people could not identify them.

Thomsen had run across the people who had attempted to salvage the car in the '70s. They claimed it was a Rollin automobile, built in Cleveland. "So, I asked, 'How did you know it was a Rollin?' but none of them could remember."

"So I went ahead and believed it was a Wisconsin-made car. The other ones were. Why would there be cars from Cleveland? It didn't make sense."

She looked at other Wisconsin possibilities like Kase. She located experts, but they could not identify them.

She learned, however, that the underside of a car is like its thumbprint. "I had the 'thumbprint.' So I looked at Rollin."

That make was only around for about a year and a half, Thomsen explained. She found a collector who kept a blog and she wrote to him "on Wednesday at 4:00 p.m. before a Thanksgiving break. When I went back in office Friday, he had written a thirteen-page thesis with pictures

The *Lakeland*'s whistle, removed from the wreck in the '60s, is on loan from the Door County Maritime Museum to Stone Harbor Resort in Sturgeon Bay. *Courtesy of Heidi Hodges.*

about why he thought these were Rollin automobiles. He climbed under cars in the museum, took pictures and matched them with those in the shipwreck. I mean, with arrows, like a play by play," said Thomsen, who was obviously impressed.

"I went out to Cleveland History Center and I met the man, Derek Moore, and he showed me a Rollin car, and he let me get in it. There are only three known existing cars. I'm pretty proud to say, we have five more of them on the bottom of Lake Michigan."

PART III

Indomitable Spirit

A Community Comes Together

World War I and the Door County Doughboys

I will go with Company F, but I will not return.
—Archie Lackshire

Sturgeon Bay's Archie Lackshire made that proclamation on a hot August day in 1917, as local boys assembled to head into the Great War—later known as World War I.

It was, tragically, prophetic. In little less than a year, Lackshire was killed in France at the Battle of Cantigny, the first Door County casualty of World War I.

Today, Sturgeon Bay's American Legion Post bears his name.

Lackshire was the first, but he wouldn't be the last. Of the 155 enlisted men and 3 officers from the company formed in Sturgeon Bay, 25 were listed as killed during the war—with many more wounded. For those men, the journey to war began in Sturgeon Bay in May 1917, with training beginning during that hot summer. They were the boys of Company F—a military unit composed of Door and Kewaunee County volunteers.

Saying Farewell

The United States had declared war just a month prior, on April 6, 1917, entering a brutal conflict that had begun three years earlier in Europe.

Shortly after the United States' declaration, Company F was formed, and a movement to organize this local unit began.

"The news had scarcely been circulated when volunteers began to appear," wrote the *Door County Advocate* in a 1969 remembrance. Ed Reynolds Jr. of Sturgeon Bay was one of the first to volunteer. "None of us boys knew what we were getting into," Reynolds told the *Advocate* in a 1980 interview. Reynolds, one of the few volunteers who already had military training, was eventually sent to officer school soon after he volunteered and was later made captain in command of Company F.

Melvin Peterson, another Company F volunteer, was quoted in the same article: "We had no idea what war was like until we were in the middle of it. We thought we were going on a camping trip. Some camping trip it turned out to be!"

Despite the initial enthusiasm, the volunteer drive was deemed "sluggish," so Sturgeon Bay's mayor, N.C. Garland, proclaimed April 14, 1917 Loyalty Day, in order for citizens to publicly demonstrate their loyalty to their country.

Over 2,500 people turned out for Loyalty Day, securing even more recruits. The local event encouraged area men to join the local unit rather than wait to be drafted. It was promoted as a means to keep in touch with the homefront "and really enjoy the outing" with friends and neighbors. In May, the men of the group were sworn into service and began military drilling exercises during the evenings, while maintaining their civilian jobs during the day.

Despite their basic organization, they were still a ragtag group, with no uniforms or equipment. Although the United States was quick to promote war propaganda—the iconic Uncle Sam "I WANT YOU" poster made its debut during World War I—it was slow to provide training and equipment.

The community stepped up to fill in the gaps and worked to accommodate the newly formed company. Men who did not live in Sturgeon Bay bunked at the high school, while city men returned to their homes in the evening.

Boy Scouts went door-to-door asking for donations of cots, mattresses and bedding for the soldiers. Local ladies prepared meals, and the Congregational Church offered its parlor as a mess hall. A ball field became the company's training ground; the men performed drills five hours each day under the command of Captain Reynolds.

And they waited, somewhat impatiently, for orders to move out to Camp Douglas in western Wisconsin. John C. Acker, a Company F man and columnist for the *Door County Democrat* newspaper, recorded in a July 1917 column, "The question of the hour is, 'When do we leave?' The men are on their toes in expectancy of the call to Camp Douglas."

In early July, Captain T.A. Watson of Fond du Lac, Wisconsin, arrived in Sturgeon Bay and took over command, while Reynolds left to attend officer's training school at Fort Sheridan in Illinois.

And then, work began in earnest. Part-time soldiering became full time. Every morning at eight o'clock, the recruits gathered at a local baseball park to learn the basics.

After training exercises were completed, the company marched a mile back to the high school, and then the hot, tired men retreated to a bar at the old Moeller Hotel (which was located on what is now Third Avenue and has since been razed) for "a good cold beer" as Querin Groessel, a Company F man from Algoma, told the *Algoma Record Herald* in a 1967 remembrance. The practice, he recalled, soon turned into a "daily ritual" that summer.

On Sundays, they often played baseball games to raise money for their "mess fund." As they formed teams of Sturgeon Bay boys versus Algoma boys, the bonds of friendship grew—acquaintances turned into friendships, and strangers bonded for life.

In late July, Captain Reynolds returned. Reynolds and two lieutenants from the Algoma area were appointed as officers attached to Company F, relieving Watson. Reynolds had his hands full. With a new bride, Reynolds returned from training and was still involved with harvesting and helping pack the last of the season's peas at the Reynolds Preserving Company, in addition to his job as head of Company F.

"I was busy as a cat on a hot tin roof," Reynolds was quoted.

The company waited to be called to Fort Douglas—the next step to eventual deployment overseas. In the meantime, Sturgeon Bay showed its hospitality with receptions, dances, banquets and excursions.

When the call to Fort Douglas finally came, the company assembled for a farewell party, arranged by a citizens' committee.

The next day, the community turned out, and the men said their farewells—some final—before the company boarded the train. According to the 1962 centennial issue of the *Door County Advocate*:

> *The flags were flying in Sturgeon Bay bright and early on Friday, August 17, 1917. And Cedar St (now Third Ave.) was lined with people all the way to the Ahnapee and Western Railroad Depot, the crowd no doubt the largest in the history of the county.... They had been drawn to Sturgeon Bay to say farewell to sons, grandsons, brothers and sweethearts who that morning were to take their first move toward the battlefields of World War I.*

The men of Company F during training at Fort Douglas in western Wisconsin, 1917. *Courtesy of Door County Historical Museum.*

LES TERRIBLES

The company received uniforms and trained at Camp Douglas as part of the First Wisconsin—and dealt with rivalries from other Wisconsin companies before shipping out to Camp MacArthur in Waco, Texas.

At Camp MacArthur, the men's fears were realized when the company was split up to fill other ranks or other regiments. Approximately two-thirds were reassigned to the 128th Infantry, and Captain Reynolds—and the other officers from the company—were given assignments away from the men.

On February 2, 1918, the Sturgeon Bay and Algoma soldiers left Waco, Texas, for Camp Merritt, New Jersey. Two weeks later, they sailed to France, where they were separated again, with privates going to the First Division and the rest of what was left of the company joining the Thirty-Second Division.

The first major battle the American troops were involved in was the horrific Battle of Chateau-Thierry, in France.

According to Captain Reynolds, they were transported to the front in the dead of the night and were warned to expect a poison gas attack from the Germans, so they prepared with their gas masks. Unfortunately for the Germans, the attack did not go as planned. Instead, many Germans died from inhaling their own chlorine gas.

Men from Company F ultimately fought in storied Battles of the Marne, Soissons, St. Michael and the Argonne.

Although forbidden to reveal details about the battles in their letters home, they shared what they could, even managing to keep the tone upbeat. In a letter to his parents, Jim Langemak wrote:

> *I was out in No Man's Land, ate some very fine blackberries while out there as it was daylight, dodged some "minnies"* [a German trench mortar], *saw some air scraps, was bombed by aircraft nearly every night that I was up there, and put my feet on the Fatherland.*

But soon the tone of his letter became more serious, as Langemak wrote of his difficulty in trying to locate the "home boys" of Company F who had been transferred to a different unit. When he finally found an old Company F friend, they shook hands and reminisced until his friend pulled a picture of his sister out of his pocket, which, according to Langmak, "made us both so blame lonesome that most of the things that we might have talked about and over were left unsaid."

Ultimately, there were decorations and recognitions for the prevailing troops. One member was awarded the Distinguished Service Cross. Another was captured by Germans but, although stabbed in the back, managed to escape.

The inexperienced boys who so eagerly enlisted in Sturgeon Bay became seasoned soldiers on the western front. Their division earned the distinction of being one of the toughest, nicknamed *Les Terribles* by the French because they were able to penetrate the German defensive line during each battle.

On April 8, the surviving company members returned home.

LAST MAN CLUB

The closeness of the company never wavered. Each year, on the August 17 anniversary of when the company left Sturgeon Bay, survivors reunited. It was always the same format: a nice meal with cocktails but no formal speeches, just reminiscing and the telling of a few jokes. Ever mindful of those who were no longer with them, they honored the memories of those who were killed in action as well as those who passed on after the war.

In 1982, six of the ten living members—who were in their mid- to late eighties then—were healthy enough to get together for their sixty-fifth reunion. As their numbers dwindled, they began calling themselves the "Last Man Club" and put away a bottle of wine for the last surviving member to drink.

In 1986, Jack Weitermann and Melvin Peterson met for dinner to celebrate their sixty-ninth reunion and to toast those who were no longer with them. They offered "get well" toasts to Captain Ed Reynolds, Grover Eichinger and William Zivney—members of the Last Man Club who were too ill to attend.

According to an *Advocate* article covering the reunion, both Weitermann and Peterson agreed their memories of the Great War were still vivid, but one memory trumped them all. "We can still remember how good it felt to come home," said Peterson. "I've never wanted to go back."

Melvin Peterson, the last surviving member from Company F, died in 1991 at the age of ninety-seven. Sadly, there is no record of what ultimately happened with the last bottle of wine.

Maybe he was too ill to enjoy it. Maybe he was saving it for the seventy-fifth anniversary.

Maybe it was because after remaining close for decades—after his Company F companions trained together, fought together and celebrated life together all those decades—it wouldn't have been fitting for him to drink it alone.

WAIL OF ANGUISH

Sturgeon Bay was in a panic. Businesses closed their doors. Most residents were out of work and still waiting for last month's pay. Food supplies were scarce. Then things got worse.

Winter came early.

If only it hadn't been such a difficult year. Still reeling from the Panic of 1857, the United States was feeling the effects of its first depression—failed banks, bankrupt railroads and ruined businesses were commonplace throughout the Midwest.

Newly organized Sturgeon Bay—then called Otumba—was not immune to this economic downturn. Lumber mills, the mainstays of this small pioneer town, saw a precipitous drop in lumber prices, forcing massive layoffs and leaving them without cash to make payroll. Mill employees and their families had to be content with clothing and food supplies from the mill stores in lieu of wages. Their wages, management said, would be delivered via the next steamship.

Door County—still wild, with dense forests, no roads and no shipping canal—relied on water navigation for almost all of its supplies. During most of the year, a steamer from Chicago made a weekly trip up Lake Michigan, around the Door Peninsula and down to Green Bay, stopping at the port of Sturgeon Bay to deliver food staples, mail and newspapers to this community of two hundred inhabitants.

In November 1857, the steamer *Ogontz* was loaded with Sturgeon Bay's winter supplies. Days earlier, however, a powerful winter storm had hit, and the bay began to freeze.

Desperate for their supplies—food staples to get the community through the winter—the men, women and children of Sturgeon Bay flocked to the mill dock to welcome the steamer and help unload cargo. Excitement and hope hung in the air when the steamer came into sight at the mouth of the bay.

Until they saw the steamer stop. And then turn around.

Not built to forge a way through the ice, *Ogontz* had no choice but to back up.

At that moment, a "wail of anguish went up from these unfortunate people," the *Door County Advocate* recounted in April 1889. Everyone, including the captain and crew of the steamer, knew these settlers would have to return home from the port to empty cupboards, not knowing when they would be full again.

They knew it would be weeks before the ice became sturdy enough to bear the weight of a horse-drawn wagon to head to Green Bay for supplies. So, Sturgeon Bay was cut off—no mail, no newspapers and, worst of all, no food. Soon, the men, women and children of the fledgling city would be starving.

Aware of the desperate situation faced by the pioneers, the *Ogontz* continued back up the bay and dropped the supplies as close as possible, near Egg Harbor, fourteen miles north of Sturgeon Bay. When word reached the people of Sturgeon Bay, they were no doubt relieved. Until they remembered they had a different problem.

No road existed between Sturgeon Bay and Egg Harbor.

According to *Door County Advocate* archives, Lyman Bradley, owner of one of the town's lumber mills, vowed to "find a way, or make it" to Egg Harbor to retrieve the supplies. It probably wasn't difficult to find a team of willing recruits. The men immediately set to work cutting a path through the thick forests and swampy wetlands.

Going was slow, though, and soon the weather turned and it began to rain. Navigating through the slushy woods in the rain, it took several days to reach their destination—the men were forced to make camp each night deep in the woods.

At last they completed a crude road connecting the two villages. Transporting the supplies was a lengthy process—the horse teams and wagons had to maneuver through the dense swampy areas and could only carry a few hundred pounds each trip. According to the *Door County Advocate*, the work proceeded so slowly, "teams were engaged throughout the entire winter in the transfer."

Yet the delivery of supplies did not provide relief for all residents of Sturgeon Bay. Supplies were rationed throughout the winter to mill employees

Illustration of the residents of Sturgeon Bay waiting on the mill dock for supplies from the steamer *Ogontz* in November 1857. *Illustration by Susie Woldt. Courtesy of* Door County Magazine.

only. Those not employed by the mill faced near starvation—most subsisted on a daily diet of molasses and potatoes (the only home-grown crop at the time).

In spite of—or maybe because of—these distressing circumstances, the people of Sturgeon Bay drew close during the winter of 1857–58.

"With feet as light as their stomachs were empty, these people had frequent dancing parties," the *Advocate* recalled in December 1882. Whenever a family received an extra bit of food, they made it an occasion to celebrate—inviting their neighbors to come and enjoy it with them. The settlers endured by coming together. There were, in fact, no mentions of starvation deaths, despite the meager supplies.

An Accident Waiting to Happen

Everyone knew it would happen eventually. The only question was when.

With only one bridge, the Steel Highway Bridge (known today as the Michigan Street Bridge), connecting the west side of Sturgeon Bay to the east side and to the rest of northern Door County, it was only a matter of time before something happened—a mechanical failure or an accident—to disable the bridge and strand the majority of Door County's population—approximately twenty thousand inhabitants—on a virtual island.

It happened on October 21, 1960.

By all accounts, bridge tender Fritz Van Duyse was having a routine Friday morning. A few minutes before 10:30 a.m., he opened the draw of the Steel Highway Bridge for a Swedish freighter—the *Carlsholm*, which was traveling from Green Bay, cutting through the Sturgeon Bay Ship Canal and heading south to Muskegon, Michigan. While waiting for the ship to pass through the open span, he happened to glance out of the window and catch sight of the massive bow heading straight toward the bridge tender house. According to the *Door County Advocate*, Van Duyse ran for his life, "waving for motorists parked on the bridge to follow his example." Most of the people on the bridge had already exited their vehicles and were running for the shore themselves.

Although the *Carlsholm* was able to maneuver at the last minute in order to miss crashing directly into the bridge tender house, its bow did collide with the draw mechanism. Witnesses—including city employees working on

Aerial photo showing both the Railroad Bridge and the Steel Highway Bridge, circa 1960. *Courtesy of Door County Historical Museum.*

a sewer construction project on the east end of the bridge—saw the draw mechanism shudder upon impact and watched as Van Duyse sprinted down the bridge toward land. They later gave Van Duyse a gift to commemorate the day—a roll of toilet tissue.

Upon hearing the first report of a boat hitting the bridge, reporters at the *Advocate* were blasé. They assumed it was the oft-rammed railway bridge, which, according to the *Advocate*, was a bridge that seemed "to leap out of its way to collide with ships."

Several theories arose as to how this collision could have happened. One theory suggested that because the *Carlsholm* was running without cargo and was therefore lighter than usual, it was at the whim of strong winds and churning waves, which contributed to its veering off course.

But another theory probably hit closer to the truth. According to an anonymous letter—which was signed "Robinson Crusoe"—published in the *Advocate* just four days after the disaster, the author blamed the "archaic railway bridge," which stood just three hundred feet from the bridge. This author

Damaged *Carlsholm* being towed for repairs after striking the Steel Highway Street Bridge in October 1960. *Courtesy of Door County Historical Museum.*

maintained that when a five-hundred-foot oceangoing freighter attempted to negotiate "the ridiculous turn" between the two bridge openings, which were at different angles and latitudinal spaces, it was a near-impossible endeavor—especially for sea captains inexperienced with local waters.

Unfortunately, this "accident that was waiting to happen" damaged the draw mechanism so severely that it could not close—even for pedestrian traffic. Initially, attempts were made to crank down the draw by hand so pedestrians could still cross the bridge, but the gap was still too great.

For seventy-three years, Sturgeon Bay had been a one-bridge town without a major incident. Suddenly, the city had to scramble to find alternatives for crossing the bay.

Desperate folks found their own way. Alice Lemens, nine months pregnant and in labor, was on her way to the hospital shortly after the *Carlsholm* crash. Unfortunately, she lived on the west side, and the Memorial Hospital was on Sturgeon Bay's east side. According to the newspaper, she called several friends who owned boats but was unable to reach them. Instead, she was forced to take a small excursion boat across the bay to a waiting ambulance. Her fourth child was born just three hours later at Memorial Hospital.

BRIDGES AND FERRIES

Early Sturgeon Bay pioneers weren't in favor of a bridge across the bay—even though it took, according to the *Door County Advocate*, eleven extra hours for a team of oxen to drive around the head of the bay and cross the portage near Lake Michigan to travel from one side of Sturgeon Bay to the other. Even when workers began digging the canal through the existing portage in 1872—and therefore making the east side of Sturgeon Bay (and the northern part of the county) a true island—a referendum to build a bridge across the bay only received eighty-two votes out of the seven hundred Door County inhabitants who voted on the issue.

By 1873, Robert Noble, a hardy pioneer who a few years earlier had lost the lower portion of both legs from frostbite, saw a business opportunity in the making. He began building a steam ferry to transport pedestrians and wagons across the bay. After the ice went out of the bay in the spring of 1874, Noble's ferry business began in earnest. Fares were five cents per pedestrian and twenty-five cents per loaded wagon with a team of two horses.

For the next decade, crossing the bay was accomplished in two ways: via the ice during the cold weather or via ferry during the warm months. That is, until two astute businessmen, John Leathem and Tom Smith, recognizing that their lumber business would soon cease to exist, started searching for a new business venture and offered to build a toll bridge across the bay. The county had looked into building a bridge a few years earlier but tabled the idea after it deemed the $16,000 to $18,000 price tag too high.

In 1887, the Leathem and Smith Toll Bridge was completed, and it soon put Robert Noble's ferry out of business. Before long, Sturgeon Bay residents were marveling at how convenient and easy it was to cross the bay and wondering how they had done without a bridge for so long.

In the early 1900s, the Ahnapee & Western Railway extended its service to Door County, and the toll bridge was shared with the railway until 1931, when the Steel Highway Bridge was completed for pedestrian and vehicle traffic. After the completion of this new bridge, the Leathem and Smith bridge was used solely for the railroad.

A COMMUNITY STRANDED

Given that it was the tail end of the tourist season and a Friday, the *Carlsholm* collision caused a bottleneck of traffic waiting to make the crossing to the east side and the journey farther north. Many decided to park their cars on the west side and took advantage of the excursion and private boats that offered to transport passengers to the other side for a fee.

By 7:00 p.m. that evening, the Washington Island ferry line had sent two of its three ferries to Sturgeon Bay to provide transportation across the bay, which the state highway commissioner had readily approved at a cost of thirty-five dollars per hour. Still, traffic was backed up seven blocks or more, and many vehicles waited up to six hours to make the crossing while logistical arrangements were made for ferry landings.

Vernon Bushman, president of the Ahnapee and Western Railway, was contacted by the city for permission to use the railway company's dock on the west side as a ferry landing. Bushman approved the use of the dock at a cost of ten dollars per hour. Crews scrambled to construct temporary gravel loading ramps on both sides of the bay and install utility lights.

This system worked well for a few days, but on Monday, October 24, Bushman demanded that any semi–tractor trailer truck using the west side ferry landing must pay a freight rate of five and a quarter cents per one hundred pounds of cargo, claiming that freight trucks were in competition with the railroad. The city halted all semi-trucks from crossing via ferry until the legal implications could be worked out—which Mayor Stanley Greene called "extortion" by Bushman.

This freight rate imposed by A&W Railway caused considerable concern in the county. The Fruit Growers Cooperative reported that it had approximately one million pounds of apples stored outside its Sister Bay plant, waiting for a shipment of glass jars so that they could be processed into applesauce. If freight trucks could not deliver the glass jars within a few days, the cooperative was facing a large financial loss—especially given that the weather was turning unseasonably cold.

Meanwhile, the Washington Island ferries, which were running twenty-four hours a day nonstop, were beginning to show signs of wear. Their engines were encountering problems from idling so much, and the steel decks were getting bent by heavy vehicles.

One bright spot was that by Tuesday, October 25, crews were able to construct steps on the pedestrian path to accommodate the large gap between the two spans so people could cross the bridge on foot. Vehicle traffic was

The *Carlsholm* continuing on its way after the collision with the Steel Highway Bridge. *Courtesy of Door County Historical Museum.*

more complicated. State officials and local work crews determined that it would take approximately three weeks to repair the damaged bridge enough so that vehicles could again cross the bridge.

City officials met with state highway officials in an emergency meeting to discuss other options for crossing the bay while the bridge was being repaired. Owing to the complications with Bushman and the use of the A&W Railway dock, they decided to discontinue use of that dock as a ferry landing. Instead, crews worked around the clock to construct a temporary dock on city property on the west side.

Officials also decided they would build a temporary bridge using a barge in the canal so the ferries could be given a break and traffic could cross the bay with fewer delays.

However, creating the barge bridge in the canal was no easy task. Roads had to be constructed on both sides of the bay leading up to the canal. On the west side, that meant one mile of scrub brush had to be removed and several loads of gravel brought in to build up the sandy soil so that it could withstand vehicle traffic.

On the east side, it was a much easier task—it was a short distance from the canal to the closest road. Still, the detour from the highway to the canal barge bridge meant that vehicles had to travel twelve miles out of the way.

Peterson Builders, a local shipbuilding company, provided the ninety-six-foot flat steel barge. Additional forty-foot-long linking spans were attached to each end of the barge—creating an efficient one lane bridge ready for traffic by Sunday October 30, just nine days after the collision.

Despite initial difficulties—such as an all-day heavy rain on Monday, October 31, that turned the west side road into mud and caused a delivery truck to slide off the road and tip over—the temporary canal bridge was seen as a major success. Local resident Ken McKiernan placed a sign on his barn that read, "The Miracle of Door County, Result of Co-operative Effort of State, County, and City Officials & Civic Minded Citizens Door County, Miracle Bridge Built in 4 days."

On the evening of November 8—almost three weeks after the *Carlsholm* collision, with repair crews working nearly around-the-clock for over two weeks—the Steel Highway Bridge was reopened, almost a week sooner than expected.

And perhaps Ken McKiernan was right about the canal bridge being a miracle, because the controversies and many heated battles—including a lawsuit—over the location for the new bridge caused so many delays that it would take another eighteen years for a second bridge to be completed.

The second bridge, known as the Bayview Bridge, was finally dedicated in June 1978. The Steel Highway Bridge (now called the Michigan Street Bridge) remains operational in Sturgeon Bay, after narrowly surviving an effort to replace it with a new four-lane bridge. Instead, a third bridge—the Oregon Street Bridge—was built 2008 just a few blocks away from the Michigan Street Bridge, providing a third alternative route across the bay—and a safety net—in case one of the bridges is again rendered inoperable.

PART IV

PLACES

Where History Was Made

Old Rugged Cross

Next to the quaint and unassuming Friends Church on Maple Street in Sturgeon Bay sits an equally unassuming memorial—an old, rugged cross, affixed with a plaque.

The cross is a dedication to an event that took place in the early twentieth century: the first performance of the popular Christian hymn "The Old Rugged Cross."

According to the Friends Community Church's website history, an early January evening in 1913 caused such a stir at the church, "the original parties who took part in this great drama submitted notarized statements and testimonies as to the details of the event."

"One of the highlights of Quaker history in this area occurred in the winter of 1912–13," wrote Reverend Eastman in the special 1962 centennial issue of the *Door County Advocate.* Eastman explained, "After Christmas, and through the first weeks of January 1913, Reverend George Bennard and his song leader, Reverend Edward E. Mieras, held a series of evangelistic meetings at the church."

Bennard, a pastor who had traveled to Sturgeon Bay, had been working on his hymn "The Old Rugged Cross" before arriving in town for the anticipated meetings. Once here, it was reported that he finished the last three stanzas—thus completing the hymn.

According to the Friends Church's history, after working on the hymn, humming it and putting on finishing touches during a dinner, Bennard and Mieras sang the hymn at the meeting, with Pearl Torstenson Berg

Opposite: Plaque affixed to the cross dedication at the Friends Church in Sturgeon Bay, erected in honor of when the hymn "Old Rugged Cross" was first performed. *Courtesy of Heidi Hodges.*

Right: A dedication to the evening the popular hymn "Old Rugged Cross" was performed for the first time. The dedication stands in the Friends Church yard on the west side of Sturgeon Bay. *Courtesy of Heidi Hodges.*

Below: Friend's Church on Sturgeon Bay's west side. *Courtesy of Heidi Hodges.*

accompanying them on organ. The church was packed with over three hundred eager listeners.

It was immediately hailed. One review of the song noted the reason for its popularity is because the hymn deviated from others regularly sung by congregations. Unusual at the time, the lyrics expressed the Christian journey, instead of simply adoration of God.

The hymn grew in popularity across the country, and an honorary monument was erected at the church on the west side of Sturgeon Bay in 1946. "Every year, several thousands of people look at the huge wooden cross and remember again the words of this great hymn," wrote Eastman.

The plaque on the cross outside the church reads:

The most popular and widely accepted Christian hymn, The Old Rugged Cross, completed by Rev George Bennard during evangelistic meetings here Dec. 29, 1912–Jan 12, 1913. First sung as a quartet in the Friends Church parlors and as a duet at the last service from penciled words and notes.

In 1947, the Reverend John Baxter published the book *The Story of the Old Rugged Cross at Sturgeon Bay, Wisconsin*. But there is a bit of controversy attached to the hymn. In actuality, three midwestern towns lay claim to it: Sturgeon Bay in Wisconsin and Albion and Pokegon in Michigan.

But the credit can perhaps be shared. Bennard was said to have started writing it in Albion, Michigan, after being ridiculed at a revival meeting. He finished the hymn in Sturgeon Bay and first performed it here. Then, that following summer, it was officially unveiled and performed in Pokegon. So, perhaps all three have an important stake in the hymn's origins.

Indeed, some versions of the song's history give little or no mention of Sturgeon Bay, since the performance was not official. But the crowd of over three hundred who attended the performance in Sturgeon Bay said they would never forget that moment.

People's Hospital

Even the hardiest of pioneers sometimes needed medical care—and the early residents of Sturgeon Bay were no exception. Still, in the early 1850s, the village of Sturgeon Bay didn't boast enough residents to maintain a full-time physician.

By 1856, Sturgeon Bay's burgeoning lumber business changed all that. Dr. Edward Battershill, the first resident physician in Sturgeon Bay, was kept busy treating sawmill employees who met with unfortunate accidents. When the sawmills closed during the Panic of 1857, however, they took with it Dr. Battershill's business.

But, as most enterprising pioneers of his day, he proved he was both flexible and resilient—he became Sturgeon Bay's combination sheriff and jailer instead.

In lieu of traditional physicians, naturopathic and women's specialty providers stepped in to fill the void. Lottie Cahoon advertised her homeopathic services in the 1862 *Door County Advocate*. She announced that, as there were no longer any practicing physicians in the area—and since she had been successfully treating her own family members and Sturgeon Bay residents for some time—she had decided to officially set up practice. Cahoon's ad also announced she would begin charging two shillings per prescription, noting that those unable to pay would receive their medicines "gratuitously as before."

Cahoon continued to advertise her services in the local newspapers for the next few years but began using the less gender-specific name C.C. Cahoon (her full name being Charlotte C. Cahoon) rather than Lottie, as she had in previous advertisements. Perhaps she felt she would be taken more seriously as a professional healthcare provider and appeal to male patrons if she used her initials instead of her actual name.

Soon after Cahoon availed Sturgeon Bay of her homeopathic services, Mrs. J.R. Mann also established herself as a provider of healthcare services specifically for women. Her ad read that she would attend to "all cases of midwifery," but like all good pioneer entrepreneurs, she also had a sideline, namely, "plain and fancy sewing by machine."

For the next thirty years, Sturgeon Bay saw its share of women's healthcare providers come and go. In 1876, Eleanor Sprang advertised as a "Physician, Surgeon, and Midwife" who had graduated from a "first class medical college in Germany." Similarly, in 1887, Anna M. Dehos sought clients for her midwifery practice, indicating she had graduated from a female medical college in Chicago. Both women practiced out of their homes in Sturgeon Bay.

General physicians came and went during this time, but unfortunately for one Door County resident, Sturgeon Bay was between doctors when he needed one the most. In December 1863, Robert Noble developed a severe case of frostbite after attempting to cross Death's Door in a small boat during a winter storm. By June of the following year, he was in desperate need of a doctor to attend to his frostbitten legs and feet.

As was most often the case with serious illness or major surgeries, Door County residents had to travel to Green Bay or farther for life-saving treatment. Transportation could take months to arrange. Fortunately for Noble, Dr. Farr—a physician from southern Wisconsin—was in Sturgeon Bay to inquire about purchasing a sawmill. Noble met with the doctor, who agreed to perform the amputation at the Cedar Street House with a saw borrowed from a local butcher.

Soon after this incident, the community realized that it needed to recruit a doctor who could set up permanent residence in Sturgeon Bay to meet the healthcare needs of the growing village, which had doubled in size since the previous January. A fund of $1,000 was raised to secure a new doctor—a Frenchman named Dr. Pommier. His tenure lasted only two years, but during that time, he developed a specialty: removing tapeworms, which he kept on display in large glass jars in his office.

As Sturgeon Bay grew, more doctors set up practice in the area. Dr. Despin, who later started a pharmacy, and Dr. Young, who established a clinic in his home, soon followed. Within twenty years, in 1886, Sturgeon

Bay boasted four resident physicians: Dr. Mullen, Dr. Cook, Dr. Hendricks and Dr. Sibree.

Of all of Sturgeon Bay's earliest physicians, it was Dr. Sibree who made the biggest impact. In 1902, Sibree established Sturgeon Bay's first hospital on what is now Memorial Drive. His Bay Shore Hospital and Sanitarium was state-of-the-art for its time, a three-story building with a large veranda, two full-time nurses, an operating room, several doctor's offices, patient rooms on the third floor and living quarters for both the maintenance crew and the cook.

For almost a decade, Dr. Sibree attended to patients, operated as hospital administrator, and paid for maintenance costs out of his own pocket. By 1911, when a citizen's group who favored a publicly-owned general hospital put in an offer to buy, Dr. Sibree was ready to give up the stress of both managing and financing the hospital. The new ownership established a board of directors, sold shares and changed the name to the People's Hospital.

During the next eight years, Dr. Sibree continued to practice medicine in Sturgeon Bay and at People's Hospital. According to his 1923 obituary, he also served as surgeon for the railroad and as city health officer, all the while still maintaining a large private practice.

The People's Hospital, located on what is now Memorial Drive in Sturgeon Bay, established by Dr. Sibree, 1902. *Courtesy of Door County Historical Museum.*

Dr. G.R. Egeland's headstone at Bayside Cemetery in Sturgeon Bay. Dr. Egeland founded a hospital in Sturgeon Bay in 1914, in competition with People's Hospital. *Courtesy of Heidi Hodges.*

People's Hospital had a short tenure as a publicly held facility. In 1914, just three years after the citizens' group bought People's Hospital from Dr. Sibree, it changed hands yet again. Apparently, the competition from a new hospital—Egeland Hospital, founded in 1914 by a physician of the same name—and the upkeep for People's Hospital had proven too costly. Dr. Hilton purchased the People's Hospital and promised to have it "thoroughly overhauled" and in "first-class condition in a short time."

By then, the glory days of Sturgeon Bay's first hospital were over. Just six years after he took ownership, Dr. Hilton was ready to turn over the reins to someone else. Once again, the community was making plans for a public hospital, the hope being to make use of the People's Hospital building until they could build a new facility. But when those plans fell through, a group of doctors—including Dr. Sibree and Dr. Hilton—pooled their resources to keep People's Hospital open. With this new venture, they renamed People's Hospital the Physicians and Surgeons Hospital. This association of doctors promised extensive renovations—at an expense of $25,000—including building a cottage on the grounds to house the kitchen and nursing quarters so that the hospital could accommodate more patients.

Maybe it was the extensive renovations or the competition from Dr. Egeland's hospital, but the Physicians and Surgeons Hospital ran into financial trouble within the next few years. By 1928, the hospital was in foreclosure, and soon after, the building was abandoned.

In 1942, Captain John Roen bought the property, razed the forlorn building and built a new home on the site.

Ironically, it was Captain Roen who pledged $25,000 for the new hospital drive in 1961, when once again, plans to build a modern general hospital were underway. That effort eventually became what is today known as Door County Medical Center—a long way from a visiting doctor and a borrowed butcher's saw.

Lover's Leap

By all accounts, it was picturesque.

Lover's Leap, a limestone ledge that hung over the rocky shore of the bay near Sherwood Point, was a mecca for both tourists and locals, who spent lazy summer days picnicking and enjoying the shade of the overhang as they watched the waves breaking on shore. Many chiseled their names into cliff walls made even more romantic by the story of how Lover's Leap got its name.

According to an article in the 1912 *Door County Democrat*, the legend was based on the story of a "young brave of the Chippewa Indians" who fell in love with the "beautiful daughter of his chief." Unfortunately, when the young brave asked for permission to be united with the chief's daughter, he was refused because he was not of "royal blood." The story published in the *Door County Democrat* continues:

> *This refusal drove the lovers to desperation. After seeking time after time to win the old chief's permission, but all in vain, the lovers decided to end it all. It is told on a beautiful, quiet, moonlit night, the brave and the princess stole from their teepees to the edge of the high cliff, where, wrapped in each other's arms in a last long embrace, the lovers leaped from the cliff to the wave-washed rocks below.*

As much as it wasn't meant to be for the young Native American brave and his princess, it also wasn't meant to be for the precipice named after

Lover's Leap near Sherwood Point. The overhanging rock fell into the bay in June 1912. *Courtesy of Door County Historical Museum.*

the legend of their ill-fated love. On another quiet, moonlit night in June 1912, the overhang unceremoniously crashed into the rocky beach below. The *Door County Democrat* reported that "the noise and jar of the breaking rock was as of an earthquake in the immediate vicinity."

The noise was so dramatic, in fact, it woke William Cochems, the light keeper from nearby Sherwood Point Lighthouse, who went out to investigate early the next morning. According to the *Democrat,* he was the first to discover the "ruin of the famous ledge."

Lover's Leap had been the scene of a picnic for seventy-five of the graduating seniors of Sturgeon Bay High School just the afternoon and the evening before it crumbled, leading the *Democrat* to surmise that it was "By the rarest good luck that the fall occurred at an hour of the night when no one was beneath the rock."

Rare good luck, indeed.

Granary

On April 24, 1906, Sturgeon Bay was galvanized by the catastrophic earthquake in San Francisco. Over 80 percent of the California city was destroyed in the quake and the resulting fire. Hundreds, if not thousands were killed. Hundreds of thousands more were left homeless.

"The hearts of Sturgeon Bay and Door County people have been touched by the terrible suffering of the people of San Francisco, who have been made homeless by the earthquake and fire which have practically swept the city out of existence," the *Door County Democrat* reported in its April 28, 1906 edition.

The city rolled up its sleeves and got to work.

> *A* [train] *car now stands on the Teweles & Brandeis sidetrack which is being loaded with provisions for the needy people of San Francisco, contributed by the people of Sturgeon Bay, and the farmers of Door County. As soon as the project was made known, the response was most liberal. The first contributor was the Jennings Packing Co. which responded with 34 cases of canned peas. Other contributions followed rapidly, and the big car will be well filled when it starts on its western trip Monday morning.*

Despite the distance of over two thousand miles, Sturgeon Bay and Door County responded with donations of flour, beans, peas, potatoes, cheese and anything that was not perishable.

The historic Teweles & Brandeis Granary on Sturgeon Bay's west side waterfront. *Courtesy of Heidi Hodges.*

At the center of the action was the Teweles & Brandeis Granary on Sturgeon Bay's west side.

The granary, which had been located adjacent to the city's steel bridge, began its life in 1901 on a dock built by Henry Harris, Joseph Harris Sr.'s son. Charles Martin purchased the dock from Harris and began building in the late 1800s. Martin went missing in July 1894 in what was likely a freak boating accident somewhere between Green Island in Green Bay and Sturgeon Bay. The dock was transferred in ownership to Martin's father-in-law, A.W. Lawrence, who had the granary built.

The local papers frequently wrote updates about the granary's development and success. In 1903, the company Teweles & Brandeis purchased the grain elevator and operated it until 1953, when it was transferred to the Door County Cooperative. The co-op continued to use the grain elevator until 2007.

At one point, in the winter of 1944, it survived a fire that ravaged the waterfront:

> *With its full 500-gallon-per-minute capacity all forced into one stream, the coastguardsmen were able to throw a stream clear up onto the elevator*

Map of early Sturgeon Bay, circa 1893, with the granary—not yet constructed—area and dock, bottom central in image. *Courtesy of Door County Historical Museum.*

> *roof, extinguishing small flames that broke out time after time....Later in the night, the big pumper was substituted at the hydrant and the three-in-one deluge nozzle was set up to spray the whole south side of the elevator and further diminish the intense heat. Even then, fire continued to flare up between the iron sheeting and wood siding, requiring the firemen to remain constantly on the alert until 10 am Thursday.*

In the end, the granary survived and continued its work.

A fixture on the waterfront for over one hundred years, the granary was also an economic fixture in the community—through the Ahnapee & Western Railroad, it was the connection between local farmers and the rest of the world.

But folks were not thinking about local economy in April 1906. The community was concerned with the news of San Francisco's devastation. They responded with great empathy, sending all they could to the leveled city.

> *Arrangements have been made to send the* [train] *car through to its destination free of cost. It will leave here over the A. & W. road and at Casco Junction will be switched to the K.G.B. & W., and at Green Bay be transferred to the tracks of the Milwaukee & St. Paul R.R. Co. and be taken to Kansas City over that line....* [T]*he Northern Pacific will pull it*

A historic look at the Teweles & Brandeis Granary. *Courtesy of Door County Historical Museum.*

> *through to San Francisco. On the side of the car will be a banner the full length of the car, painted in large letters, "Relief car for San Francisco from Sturgeon Bay and Door County." The painting of the sign was donated by Alfred Wulf.*

A treasurer was appointed, and Sturgeon Bay's newspaper offices were designated as a spot to drop off monetary contributions. The money was used to purchase provisions that were included in the train car. "All contributions, either produce or money, large or small, will be duly acknowledged," the *Democrat* wrote, urging citizens to join the effort.

Such was the spirit of Sturgeon Bay.

In recent years, local citizens rallied around the granary, filling meeting halls and auditoriums, arguing for the structure's preservation and reuse. In late 2017, by a slim majority, the Sturgeon Bay City Council voted to demolish the granary for future development, despite it having been deemed sound and salvageable by architectural preservation experts and having been included in the Wisconsin State Register of Historic Places and the National Register of Historic Places. Bids were secured for the granary's removal, but on the eve of demolition, the granary was given

Interior photos of granary in 2015.
Courtesy of Heidi Hodges.

The 117-year-old Teweles & Brandeis Granary is afforded a chance at restoration after it was moved in March 2018 from the west side of the city to the east via the Oregon Bridge. *Courtesy of melaniejane.*

an eleventh-hour reprieve when it was agreed the structure could be moved to a development area on the other side of the bay, with plans for its restoration and future commercial and tourism-related use. In late March 2018, the granary was moved, traversing the Oregon Street Bridge in town and resting at a temporary location until a permanent site might be arranged.

Bibliography

Books

Christianson, Carl Raymond. *Ship Building and Boat Building: In Sturgeon Bay, Wisconsin from the Beginning to 1985*. Self-published, 1985.

Holand, Hjalmar. *History of Door County, Wisconsin: The County Beautiful*. Ellison Bay, WI: Wm Caxton Ltd., 1993.

Martin, Chas. I. *History of Door County, Wisconsin: Together with Biographies of Nearly Seven Hundred Families*. Sturgeon Bay, WI: Expositor Job Print, 1881.

Websites

Door County Library Rescarta, Online Newspaper Archive. http://pubinfo.co.door.wi.us:8080/jsp/RcWebBrowseCollections.jsp.

Wisconsin Historical Society, Turning Points in Wisconsin History: The Women's Suffrage Movement. https://www.wisconsinhistory.org/turningpoints/tp-032.

Friends Community Church. https://www.friendscommunitychurchsb.com/our-history.html.

Magazines

The stories titled "Bertha Falk: Widowed Immigrant Finds a New Life"; "The Pioneering Spirit of the Graham Family"; "Founding Father Joseph Harris"; "The *Lakeland*: Mystery at the Bottom of Lake Michigan"; "World War I and the Door County Doughboys"; and "Wail of Anguish" are reprinted herein, in full or in part, with the permission of *Door County Magazine* for whom they were originally written.

About the Authors

Heidi Hodges

Heidi grew up in Kenosha, Wisconsin, but spent family vacations in Door County, at Peninsula State Park, Gills Rock and at a little log cabin south of Sturgeon Bay. She received a bachelor of arts in technical communication from the University of Wisconsin–Platteville in 1988, focusing on photography and journalism. To complete her major, she interned at the *Door County Advocate* in 1987–88. She remained at the *Advocate* for thirteen years after the internship, until leaving to start her own photography and freelance writing business in 2001. In 2009, she won a National Newspaper Award for a special-issue magazine she spearheaded, *Taking Flight*, chronicling her journey through breast cancer. In 2013, she was named editor of the *Door County Magazine*, where she continues today, working her dream job of highlighting this place she's loved all her life. Heidi lives in Sturgeon Bay with her two sons, Fred and Gordon, surrounded by family, friends and lots of beautiful water.

Kathy Steebs

Kathy was born and raised in Door County, where she met and married her husband, Scott. After graduating from the University of Wisconsin–Milwaukee with a bachelor of arts in English, she worked as a technical writer in Milwaukee. In 2000, she moved back to Door County with her husband and son, Wil. In addition to freelance technical writing, she also writes for *Door County Magazine*. Kathy has been a tireless researcher of local history and finding the hidden histories of the area. Her most prized possession is a copy of Hjalmar Holand's *History of Door County, Wisconsin: The County Beautiful* she inherited from her mother-in-law, Keta Steebs.